FLOWERING
HOUSE
PLANTS

THE GARDEN LIBRARY

FLOWERING HOUSE PLANTS

Kenneth A. Beckett

BALLANTINE BOOKS · NEW YORK

Editor
Anthony Livesey

Designers
Steven Wooster
Julia Goodman

Managing Editor
Jackie Douglas

Art Director
Roger Bristow

Consultants
Margaret McQuade Hagedorn
James Fanning

First published in Great Britain in 1984 by
Dorling Kindersley Limited

The Garden Library FLOWERING HOUSEPLANTS was conceived,
edited and designed by Dorling Kindersley Limited,
9 Henrietta Street, London WC2E 8PS

Library of Congress Catalog Card Number: 83-91182

ISBN 0-345-30909-X

Manufactured in the United States of America

First Ballantine Books Trade Edition: April 1984
10 9 8 7 6 5 4 3 2 1

Contents

Care and cultivation 6
Buying: what to look for 7
Watering 7 · Humidity 8 · Feeding 8
Top-dressing 9 · Potting mixes 10
Propagation 11
Pruning, training and supporting 16
Pests and diseases 17
Temperature 17

The flowering house plants 18–94

Glossary 95

Index 95–96

Care and cultivation

The appeal of plants in the home is twofold: they embellish the decor and provide a link with the world outside. Broadly, house plants are those that will live indoors, if only for a comparatively short time. Some are more tolerant of house conditions than others and it is the most decorative of these that are popular. House plant nurserymen are continually trying out new plants to add variety and for this reason those available vary from year to year, although hardcore favorites are always obtainable.

It is surprising, considering their natural habitats, how many plants will survive in the dry atmosphere and indifferent light of the average home. There are species and varieties suitable for most sites in the house, so obtain the right plant for the position in mind and do not buy on impulse. The best sites are window-ledges, tables and shelves nearby, and room corners. In large rooms plants can also be used as dividers and in all rooms to beautify fireplaces in summer. Never keep plants near a fire, however.

Of primary importance to any plant is a source of light. Some, such as cacti, need plenty of direct sunlight, while others, such as ferns and some foliage plants from forest floors, will tolerate quite deep shade. However, there are very few flowering plants that will stand shade for long.

For dark corners there are two choices: to work a shuttle system from a sunny or well-lit window, or to install an artificial lighting unit. In the first case, two or more plants are needed, one or more in a dark corner, the others on a window-ledge. They must then be changed around once a week. The other alternative is a fluorescent tube that gives adequate light but little heat. Special light units can be purchased. They may be small and simple for one plant, or more elaborate with tiers of shelves. With units of this sort, plants can be grown even in a windowless cellar. Ordinary electric light bulbs provide a supplementary source of illumination. Care must be taken, however, to ensure that the plants are not too close to the light bulbs, as they give off a lot of heat.

Artificial light can be used either to supplement normal daylight or as a substitute for it in poorly lit positions. The system below comprises a covered and circular fluorescent tube above a shallow pan, suitable for plants with small roots.

Larger versions of the small system above and those with multiple shelving are used to accommodate a greater number of plants. In all cases, the fluorescent tubes or incandescent bulbs are backed by a reflector to make the most of light power.

Buying: what to look for

Plants can be raised from seeds and cuttings but it is usual to start a collection by buying well established plants from a supermarket, nurseryman, florist or garden center. It is not easy for the beginner to identify suitable, healthy plants. The best growers of pot plants ensure that each plant has a label giving its name and the growing conditions required. Sometimes, however, less common species of plant are available locally and then a comprehensive house plant book must be consulted.

When buying a plant, the following points should be remembered. The plant must be compact and sturdy, not thin and weak with long stretches of bare stem between the leaves. The leaves should stand firmly on their stalks and not hang limply, which could mean lack of water or trouble at the roots or stem base. Unless the plant is known to have variegated leaves, the foliage should be a healthy shade of green and not yellowish. A good flowering specimen should be taller than the pot is deep and overlap the pot width. There should be plenty of flowers and buds, ideally more of the latter than the former, and when given a gentle shake few or no blossoms should fall off. Avoid a specimen that sheds flowers in abundance and always check a plant for pests before buying it. Take the plant home as soon as possible, especially in winter. Many house plants come from the tropics or sub-tropics and may drop leaves and flowers or be damaged in other ways if subjected to long periods of cold.

The best houseplant nurserymen will provide detailed instructions on how to care for a plant. Essential information includes temperature, light and watering requirements.

Poor specimen

Good specimen

Sturdy, healthy plants must be selected for the home. Look for specimens with a compact habit, well furnished with leaves that do not droop. If in bloom, make sure there are plenty of buds and that open flowers do not fall readily.

Watering

More house plants have died as a result of under- or over-watering than from any other cause. Watering, of all the cultural practices, is the most difficult to master. Frequency of watering depends upon the time of year, the temperature and the stage of the plant's development. For example, a newly potted plant with plenty of unexploited soil around the roots will need watering less frequently than one of a similar size that is pot bound (that is, when the container is filled tight with roots). Plants with stems and leaves that are growing will need more water than those that have reached maturity or are dormant.

Deciding when a plant needs watering is a matter of skill based upon experience. The aim is to keep the soil moist but not wet. Too frequent watering will result in a sour potting soil, which encourages root rot and the collapse of the plant, while too little water will slow down growth and cause leaf yellowing and bud drop. There are many

One of the most reliable methods of testing when a plant needs water is to scratch with a finger into the surface of the potting mix to about ½ in (1 cm). If the mix feels barely moist, water without delay.

Most plants must be watered from above, filling the space between the surface of the potting mix and the rim of the container. A few plants, such as species of Saintpaulia, thrive on being watered from below by standing the container in water until the potting mix is damp.

Humidity is important to most house plants. Extra, localized humidity can be provided by standing the plants on trays of flooded gravel. The water should not reach the base of the pot.

time-honored ways of deciding when to water pot plants. One is to rap the pot with a small wooden mallet or the knuckle, a ringing tone denoting dry soil. This works reasonably well with clay pots providing they are not cracked, but not with the increasingly popular plastic pots. Hefting a pot plant has limited use and requires keen judgment as the modern all-peat potting mixes do not feel very heavy, even when really moist. The easiest method of deciding when a plant needs watering is to scratch into the soil surface with the tip of a finger. If the soil feels barely moist at a depth of about ½ in (1 cm) then give water. During the summer or in a warm room, give water if still in doubt. At other times of the year, especially in a cooler room, do not. It is safer for the plant to wilt very slightly before watering than to sit permanently in wet soil.

Having decided that watering is necessary, the job must be done thoroughly. The gap between the soil surface and the rim of the container should be filled and the water allowed to drain right through the soil. A quick dribble is likely to do more harm than good since it dampens only the top layer of soil, thus encouraging surface roots that are then vulnerable to drought. Once again, skill and commonsense must be the final arbiters.

Humidity

Many house plants originate from areas where rainfall is frequent and the air humid, at least during the growing season. Although some of these plants are surprisingly tolerant of a dry atmosphere, they grow more successfully in a humid one. This can be provided by standing the plants on gravel-filled trays into which water is poured. The water level must be topped up regularly so that it comes to just below the surface of the gravel. The bottom of the pot must not sit in water or the root system will become waterlogged. There are other ways of providing humidity. Pots can be wholly or partially buried in moist peat, vermiculite or perlite in deep trays or other containers. The peat must be kept just moist but never really wet. Moistening the foliage once a day with a small hand operated mist sprayer is beneficial; alternatively, a once- or twice-weekly spraying can be given. Either way, soft or rain water should be used, for hard water leaves an unsightly white deposit on plants.

Feeding

However fertile your potting soil, sooner or later the plant roots will rob it of the main nutrients and supplementary feeding becomes necessary. A slow-growing plant, such as a Clivia, may not need feeding for up to a year, but a quick-growing short term subject, such as *Cineraria* or *Calceolaria*, will need it as soon as purchased or after six to eight weeks if you pot it on.

Fertilizers for pot plants are best applied in a liquid form. Numerous types are on the market and all do the job for which they are intended, but they vary greatly in price and it is wise to shop around. Always use proprietary liquid feeds to the makers' exact instructions.

Annual and biennial pot plants will need feeding about six weeks after the final potting or when flower buds show, whichever is earlier. Once feeding is started it should continue at intervals of 10–14 days, unless the makers' instructions suggest a greater frequency. Today there are dilute feeds on the market that are designed to be used at every watering. Once a short-term plant has reached the height of its flowering period, feeding can cease. Long-term plants should be fed throughout their active growth period, and those with bulbs, corms or tubers should be fed for several weeks after flowering to build up the root-stocks before drying off.

For a quick tonic as well as more regular feeding, foliar feeds are worth considering. These are highly solvent fertilizers which, when diluted in water, can be sprayed on to the leaves, where they are rapidly absorbed by the plant. They are particularly useful if the more traditional methods of feeding have been neglected and the plant needs to be brought back to health and vigor in the shortest possible time.

Top-dressing

Some long-term pot plants, particularly shrubs and climbers such as *Bougainvillea*, *Stephanotis*, *Ixora* and *Pentas*, do not need re-potting annually but need more regular doses of liquid feed and will benefit from top-dressing. This means stripping away the top layer of potting mix in the container and replacing it with fresh material. Use a small hand fork or old kitchen spoon to loosen the mix and any small roots, removing up to a quarter of the total depth of the root ball. Remove small roots with care but ensure larger ones are not damaged. Fill the gap with new potting mix, ideally containing granular, slow-release fertilizer.

Re-potting and potting-on

There comes a time in the life of a pot plant, particularly the bulbous and shrubby sorts, when it needs a change of potting mix or extra to extend root growth. This is done either by re-potting or potting-on. These terms are sometimes confused,

Top-dressing

Long-term pot plants which stay in the same container for several years benefit from top-dressing. Strip away the top layer of potting mix with a small spoon.

Remove up to a quarter of the total root ball depth, plus any small roots in the way. Replace this immediately with fresh potting mix, lightly firm and then water.

Young plants regularly need larger containers if they are to reach full size and flowering potential. This operation is known as potting-on. Remove the plant from its pot and strip off any hard surface layer from the potting mix.

Select a larger pot, place crocks and then potting mix in the bottom and position the plant. Fill round with more potting mix.

Tap the pot on a firm surface to settle the potting mix, then push the fingertips into it to firm it. If the gap is too narrow for the fingers, use a blunt stick.

even by professional nurserymen. Potting-on entails transplanting a containerized plant into a larger container. Re-potting is the removal of all or almost all potting mix from the roots and replacing the plant in the same pot or one of similar size. This operation is used for bulbous plants such as *Cyclamen* and *Lachenalia*, which lose leaves and roots when dormant, and for shrubby plants that need to be kept compact.

When potting-on, remove the plant from its pot by placing your hand across the top of the container with the stem between the first and middle fingers. Then turn the pot upside down and rap the rim firmly against a wooden surface, such as a bench or table edge. Choose a new pot that is large enough to allow ½–1 in (1–2.5 cm) of space all around the root ball. Lay gravel or pieces of broken clay pot (crocks) in the bottom of the pot to ensure good drainage and prevent potting mix from flushing through. Cover this with a layer of potting mix so that when the root ball is in place it will be covered with about ½ in (1 cm) of soil but leaving enough room for watering. Position the root ball, then carefully pour potting mix into the gap between it and the pot and push down lightly but firmly with the fingertips or a blunt stick. The gap between the surface of the mix and the rim of the container must be adequate for watering. A guide is to leave a space equal to one seventh of the total pot depth.

Re-potting is more straightforward. It should only be done when the plant is resting or dormant, usually between late summer and early spring. The plant must be removed from the container and all old potting mix crumbled away. With bulbs, corms and tubers this is simple but with woody plants (shrubs and climbers) a hand fork is necessary. Trim the root system drastically, removing about one third to a half of the roots and shake off as much soil as possible. Then re-pot the plant, using new potting mix and leaving a gap between the soil surface and pot rim for watering.

Potting mix

The vigor and health of a plant largely depends upon the potting mix. It is possible to use ordinary garden soil but it is seldom rich enough and tends to drain badly. The roots of a plant usually quest outwards and, when growing naturally, spread wider than the stems overhead in their search for water and essential nutrients. In a container, they are confined to a comparatively small volume of soil and for this reason potting mix must be richer than garden soil.

A number of carefully formulated potting mixes are available from garden centers, supermarkets and nurserymen. Composts or mixes fall into two categories, those with and those without loam. The best loam can be described as perfect soil, being a natural blend of clay, sand and organic matter. In the cooler climates of the northern hemisphere good loam is found beneath old pastures but it is now generally in short supply. In recent years, however, loamless or all-peat composts have come to the fore and are generally ideal for a wide range of pot plants.

Peat is composed of partially decayed plant remains that has formed under water. Moss peat is largely bog moss (*Spaghnum*), while sedge peat is the remains of the roots and leaves of sedges (*Carex*) and rushes (*Juncus*) formed in marshes. When properly prepared, peat is light, clean and easy to handle and, with the addition of essential minerals, makes a good rooting medium. However, all-peat mixes have certain disadvantages. If allowed to dry out they shrink drastically and pull away from the sides of the container. The plants are then difficult to water properly, for the water will run down the crack without entering the peat mix. Even when moist, peat is comparatively light. This means that large plants rooted in it become top heavy and can easily fall over. Both these faults can be overcome by the addition of coarse sand or grit, one quarter part by bulk being adequate.

Propagation

A wide variety of flowering pot plants is readily available from garden centers and florists, but there is always pleasure in raising plants from seeds or cuttings. No special equipment is needed, though plastic propagating trays and pots with rigid, transparent covers are useful. Better still are the small custom-made propagating units, with a heating element in the bottom. In a warm room most of the popular pot plants can be raised without such equipment. Pots covered by clear plastic bags or plastic food boxes with lids that admit light are perfectly adequate. A few seeds will only germinate in carefully controlled conditions.

The easiest and generally most effective rooting medium for cuttings is coarse, washed sand or perlite. By adding an equal quantity (by bulk) of moss peat, the medium will conserve moisture. Once rooted, the cuttings must be potted in proper potting soil to prevent starvation. If potting is delayed, a liquid or foliar feed must be used.

STEM CUTTINGS Also known as slips, these are severed pieces of stem, with or without leaves. Stem cuttings of houseplants fall into several categories. The first category consists of softwood

A custom-built, heated propagator often has a thermostat so that the temperature can be regulated as required (above, top). The addition of a light unit over the propagator (above) allows plants to thrive in a poorly lit position.

cuttings, young shoots just forming or the soft growing tips of older stems. The second category includes semi-hardwood cuttings, pieces of older stem already starting to get woody but still growing at the tips. The latter technique is used for shrubby or semi-shrubby plants, such as *Azalea*, *Hedera*, × *Fatshedera* and *Pentas*. A third category, hardwood cuttings, are taken from the fully matured stems of trees, shrubs and climbers, often when leafless. Among the pot plants mentioned here, only *Bougainvillea* is sometimes propagated by hardwood cuttings.

Leafy cuttings (softwood and semi-hardwood) are usually taken in spring or summer. The exact length depends on the plant species. For example, a cutting from a robust-stemmed *Pelargonium* should be about 4 in (10 cm) when trimmed, with two leaves at the top, while a thin-stemmed plant such as *Cuphea* need be no more than 1¼–1½ in (3–4 cm) long with about ten leaves. When severed from the plant, cuttings should be somewhat longer than this to allow for trimming. Cut them off with a sharp knife or pruning shears just above a node (leaf or bud). If snags of bare stem are left above a node they may die back further and spoil the appearance of the plant. Once severed from the plant, the cuttings must be planted immediately or, if necessary, stored in a jar of water or plastic bag to avoid wilting. Before planting the cutting, cut or break the leaves from the lower half of the stem, ensuring that the base is cleanly severed just below a node. To make sure of rooting and to minimize rotting, it is advisable to dip the base of each cutting in one of the proprietary rooting powders that contain a fungicide. Insert each cutting in the rooting medium with the aid of a dibber or pencil, making sure that about half of the stem is buried. The spacing of the cuttings will vary according to their size, but generally a distance apart equal to half their overall length is about right. Large cuttings, such as *Pelargonium*, are best inserted individually in small pots, while smaller cuttings, such as *Cuphea*, can be placed around the sides of pans or pots or in rows in larger containers. As each pot or box of cuttings is completed, water it with a fine-rosed can, then put it in the propagator or cover it with a plastic bag, screened from direct sunlight. However, do not enclose in this way any fleshy stemmed or leaved plants, such as *Pelargonium*, and those from arid regions, such as cacti. Such plants are best placed directly on the greenhouse bench or a window-ledge, for high humidity can encourage rotting. Living-room temperature is usually satisfactory. If a heated propagator in a greenhouse is used, a

Pelargonium cutting

warm temperature of 65–70°F (18–21°C) is adequate. Most of the hardier plants will root in slightly cooler temperatures. The time taken to root varies with the species but two to four weeks is about the average, with some of the more woody-stemmed plants taking longer. Once rooted and starting to grow again, the cuttings must be carefully separated and placed singly in containers of potting mix.

LEAF CUTTINGS Some flowering pot plants, notably species of *Saintpaulia*, *Begonia* and *Streptocarpus*, can be increased by using single leaves or leaf sections as cuttings. Small-leaved species of *Begonia* and *Saintpaulia* are grown from whole leaves, each with a short length of stalk. About half of the stalk should be inserted in a rooting medium. Leaves of large-leaved begonias must be removed without a stalk. Pierce the main veins with the point of a knife at ¾ in (2 cm) intervals. Lay the leaf on the rooting medium and, if it does not sit flat, anchor it with small pebbles or hairpins. Plantlets will develop at the nicks and can be separated and potted when they have two or three leaves. An alternative method is to cut the leaf into ¾–1 in (2–2.5 cm) squares and lay them on the soil surface. Enclose them in a propagating case or plastic bag to keep the leaf cuttings humid.

New begonia plantlets can be grown from leaf cuttings. A whole leaf, nicked across the veins with a knife point (top), or cut into squares about 1 in (2 cm) across (above), are laid on the surface of the potting mix. New plantlets arise from the slit veins.

LAYERING This is the practice of stimulating a stem to root while still attached to the parent plant. It is mainly used on climbers such as *Jasminum*, or shrubs such as *Ficus*, with flexible stems. One- or two-year-old stems should be chosen, which can be easily bent down to a prepared pot of seed-sowing or potting mix. Bend the stem into a 'U' shape and nick or slice almost halfway through the stem at the point where it will touch the potting mix. Dust the wound with rooting powder and bury the base of the 'U' ¾–1¼ in (2–3 cm) in the rooting medium. A forked twig or

Layering is a simple way of propagating climbing plants and shrubs with flexible stems. Bend the chosen stem into a 'U' shape, nick the base of the 'U' (right) and secure it in a container of potting mix with a forked stick or bent wire (below) before covering shallowly with more potting mix.

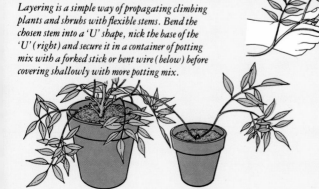

a hairpin may be needed to hold the layer in place. The free end of the layer, if long and flexible, is best secured to a small cane. Rooting can take three to six months, sometimes longer. When well rooted, the layer must be severed and potted on. The severing is best done in two stages, first cutting halfway through the stem and then completely through four to six weeks later.

Where stems are rigid or it is inconvenient to bend them down, it is possible to use a technique known as air- or Chinese-layering. This method is used when tall plants such as *Tibouchina* lose their lower leaves and you want to rejuvenate the plant by shortening the main stem, or when you want to create new plants from the remaining leafless stem. The selected stem must be nicked or sliced halfway through, 6–8 in (15–20 cm) below the tip and leaves 4 in (10 cm) either side of the wound removed. If the slicing method is used, the cut must be held just open by a piece of wood or a tiny pebble. Depending on the stem thickness, a 5–8 in (13–20 cm) section of 'lay-flat' plastic tubing must be slipped over the stem and positioned so that the wound is halfway between the two ends. Secure the bottom end with insulating tape. Then fill the tube firmly with a 50–50 mixture of moss and potting or seed-sowing mix. Pure moss or moist perlite can also be used. After filling with the mix, secure the top of the tube in the same way as the bottom end. When a good network of roots is visible, the layer can be severed and potted. It is usually advisable to put newly potted layers in a partially shaded, humid position for a week or two until established.

When air layering, nick or partially slice the stem, cover with plastic sleeving and fill with potting mix and moss. When roots have formed, sever the top of the plant from the base and pot separately.

Tubers and rhizomes (below) with several 'eyes' or growing points can be divided. Do this just as they start into growth, slicing with a knife so that each section has a shoot.

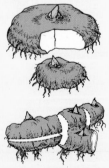

DIVISION Clump-forming plants, such as *Clivia* and *Streptocarpus*, can be divided during the cool rest period or early spring. Remove the plant from its container and shake off as much potting mix as possible. However, this will not be possible if the plant is pot-bound. Pull or slice apart the plant with a serrated knife, ensuring that each division has plenty of roots and a tuft of leaves or shoots. Divisions must be potted immediately.

Some tuberous plants can be increased by cutting the tubers into pieces just as they start into new growth. Each piece must have at least one sturdy young shoot.

OFFSETS Some plants produce smaller shoots at the base (offsets), an example being *Aechmea*. These can be removed and grown on to maturity. Bulbs such as *Hippeastrum* also produce some offsets in the form of tiny side-bulbs. These can be removed when re-potting and planted separately.

SEEDS A few flowering pot plants are regularly raised from seed, including *Cyclamen*, *Primula*, *Calceolaria* and *Cineraria*. Seeds provide a particularly fascinating and satisfactory means of increasing your favorite plant supply and are not difficult to deal with as long as the right conditions are provided. To germinate successfully and grow into healthy plants, seeds require moisture, air, the correct temperature and, when leaves expand, varying degrees of light. For sowing, either a special seed sowing mix or a sterilized potting mix is recommended as it will not contain weed seeds, which can be a real nuisance when growing ornamental plants from seed. Pots, pans, boxes and divided trays for peat pellets can be used for sowing, the size depending upon the number of seedlings required. Fill the container to within ¾ in (2 cm) of the rim, firming the surface lightly and evenly. Fine seeds, such as *Begonia*, are best mixed with several volumes of fine dry sand to ensure even dispersal.

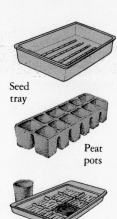

Seed tray

Peat pots

Tray with division for peat pellets

All seeds must be sown thinly and as evenly as possible, for over-crowded seedlings are prone to damping-off disease and get drawn and starved. Fine seeds do not need to be covered with potting mix, but all others must be covered with a layer of fine potting mix equal to the diameter of a seed. When sown, water the container by immersion in a tray or bowl of water, allow it to drain and then place in a propagating case or plastic bag and leave on a window-ledge. Screen the container from direct sunlight.

When seedlings appear they must be acclimatized to direct light over a period of several days. The first leaves to form are usually the seed or cotyledon leaves. These differ from the true or rough leaves, sometimes very markedly. When the

To sow a number of seeds, use either pots or trays, first putting in a layer of drainage material and then seed-sowing mix. Make shallow drills, distribute the seeds, cover with a fine layer of sowing mix and stand the container in a tray of water, briefly.

first true leaves can be seen, the seedlings are ready to prick off – that is, to space out singly, either in rows in boxes or individually in small pots. The seedlings must be carefully teased or shaken apart and planted with a dibber or widger. Depending on seedling size, set them 1–2 in (2.5–5 cm) apart each way. Water with a gentle spray and leave the seedlings in the same conditions to grow on. With some seedlings, pinching out is necessary to encourage bushiness. When the seedlings become young plants and their leaves begin to overlap, they must be separated again and potted singly.

Pruning, training and supporting

The majority of pot plants need neither pruning nor training and very little support. Some shrubby types, for example *Brunfelsia*, *Catharanthus*, *Fuchsia*, *Pentas* and *Sparmannia*, can be made bushier and more shapely if the stem tips are pinched out when young plants are 4–6 in (10–15 cm) tall. This pinching out, or stopping as it is also known, can be carried out on side branches if necessary. A few plants tend to flop, especially if they have been left in poor light. *Achimenes*, *Kohleria* and *Smithiantha* are examples. These can be held up with small twiggy sticks pushed in around the perimeter of the container, or by split canes, ideally stained green. Whatever the method, do it neatly and as unobtrusively as possible for nothing detracts more from the beauty of a pot plant than ugly staking.

Climbing, tall-growing or weak-stemmed plants normally need supporting. Slim bamboo canes and spills are the most useful for this purpose, those dyed green being least obtrusive.

Climbing plants are the primary exceptions to these comments. All need supporting and the more vigorous sorts must be regularly pruned. Although specially designed supports can be bought, they are seldom entirely satisfactory. Better to grow small-growing species over a balloon of thick, galvanized wires, and to wind taller ones around three or four canes pushed in near the edge of the pot. Twining climbers will cling without aid but the non-twiners will need tying in at intervals, ideally with a green plastic or string tie.

Perennial and woody-stemmed climbers, such as *Bougainvillea*, *Dipladenia*, *Jasminum*, *Manettia*, *Passiflora* and *Plumbago*, need pruning at least once a year, the best time being in winter. Once the support is covered with a framework of main stems, pruning consists of thinning out and shortening all the lateral stems. Where these are congested, some can be cut out completely or reduced to short stubs or spurs. Others can be cut back by a half to two-thirds. Failure to carry out annual pruning can result in a wild tangle which can be a labor to deal with. For this reason, you must never be afraid to wield the pruning shears.

Pests and diseases

Plants in the home are fortunately prone to very few pests and diseases and those that develop are usually on the plants when obtained. Apart from the pests listed below, most troubles arise from cultural mismanagement, in particular over- and under-watering, starvation and lack or excess of sunlight and room heat. The following pests are the most likely to be troublesome. A wide variety of chemical preparations to combat them can be obtained and new ones come on the market continually. As the newer ones tend to be less poisonous to man and more deadly to the pests, it is as well to seek advice at garden centers for the best preparations currently available. Whichever one is chosen, it must always be used strictly to the makers' instructions.

Aphids (plant lice or greenfly) are tiny, soft-bodied creatures usually crowded together on stem tips and the undersides of leaves. They suck sap and cause crippling of stems, leaves and flowers. Small infestations can be squashed between the thumb and forefinger or swabbed with soapy water but for larger infestations use a proprietary pesticide as required.

Red spider mites are microscopic, spider-like creatures, ranging from almost colorless to red-spotted or wholly red. Sometimes they are surrounded by a very fine webbing. They cause a yellowish freckling on the leaves and severe infestations can bring premature leaf-fall.

White flies are like minute white moths and fly when the plant is tapped. In their immature form they are even smaller, almost colorless with oval scales which suck sap. The damage is rather like that caused by the red spider mite.

Greenfly

Red spider mite

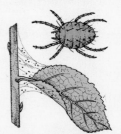

White fly

(All insects greatly magnified)

Temperature

Most plants tolerate high temperatures during the day but a great number will not survive very cool temperatures at night. In the following articles, temperature recommendations refer to the minimum tolerated by a plant. As a guide, the terms used refer to the following temperature ranges: cool 40–50°F (4–10°C); medium 50–60°F (10–16°C); warm 60–70°F (16–21°C).

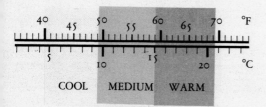

Abutilon pictum 'Thompsonii'

Abutilon

Most of the 150 species of Abutilon (flowering maple) are evergreen shrubs. Those used as pot plants have pleasing, maple-shaped leaves and large, nodding bell flowers on slender stalks, which open from spring through late fall. One of the most tolerant for the home is *A. pictum* 'Thompsonii', which has yellow variegated leaves accompanying its red-veined, orange flowers. It grows to 4 ft (1.2 m).

Position *To bloom well, flowering maples must have bright light and should be placed where they get about four hours of direct sunshine daily. They require a medium temperature, minimum 50°F (10°C).*

Water and food *During active growth water regularly, maintaining the potting mix in a moist state. Apply liquid feed at two-weekly intervals from late spring through fall. Prune and top dress in late winter.*

Propagation *Stem tip cuttings about 4 in (10 cm) long root readily in spring if placed in a peat and sand or perlite mix and kept in a propagating case. They must be kept in a warm temperature, minimum 60°F (16°C).*

The best cuttings are taken from healthy side (lateral) stems (left); avoid those that are very thin. After cutting cleanly beneath a node, remove the lower two leaves. Dipping the base in a hormone rooting powder is worthwhile but not essential (top right). Cuttings can be inserted singly in small pots or several put in a larger container (right).

Achimenes hybrid

Achimenes

Known popularly as hot water plant, monkey-faced pansy and Cupid's-bower, *Achimenes* have been available as pot plants for many years. The numerous species are very different in character: for example, some are erect (e.g. *A. glabrata*), others lax or trailing (e.g. *A. candida*). The latter make excellent hanging basket plants. The summer- to fall-borne flowers also vary greatly in size and color; some are quite small, others may be 2 in (5 cm) long, in shades of red, pink, purple, orange, yellow and white. The rhizomes are strange, cone-like organs made up of tiny, fleshy scales.

Position *Bright light is vital, but during summer the plants must be screened from direct sunshine during the hottest part of the day. A medium night temperature, minimum 55 °F (13 °C), is necessary.*
Water and food *Apply water sparingly when the rhizomes are potted in spring, increasing amounts as the foliage develops; then keep potting mix moist until fall, when the rhizomes must be allowed to dry off. Apply liquid feed to actively growing plants at two-weekly intervals until flowering ceases.*
Propagation *The natural increase of rhizomes provides plenty of extra plants. Scales rubbed from the rhizomes can be sown as seed.*

Achimenes rhizomes must be handled carefully. An all-peat mix is an ideal potting mix, with or without the addition of sand or perlite. For a good display, plant three to five rhizomes in a 5 in (13 cm) pot, then cover with about 1 in (2.5 cm) of the potting mix.

Aechmea fasciata

Aechmea

Species of this tropical South American genus are mainly air plants (epiphytes), which are found in nature perching on the branches and trunks of rainforest trees. Like most epiphytes, they are well adapted to stand extreme conditions and make splendid, tough house plants. All the popular species of *Aechmea* have decoratively banded or marbled foliage, almost as ornamental as the flowers. Best known are *A. fasciata* (urn plant) and the silvery, banded-leaved *A. Chantinii*.

Position *Although tolerant of partial shade, they will only flower well where they receive several hours of direct sunlight each day. A medium night temperature, minimum 55°F (13°C), is required and high humidity in summer.*
Water and food *Water regularly during the growing season but allow the potting mix almost to dry out before rewatering. Also pour water into the cup-like center of the main rosette and replenish it from time to time. Apply liquid feed at two- to three-weekly intervals, except in winter.*
Propagation *Remove offsets from the base of mature plants in early summer.*

Offsets should be at least half the size of the parent and severed cleanly at their junction with the main stem or rosette base. Set each offset in a small pot, burying it up to the base of the lowest leaf. If necessary, secure it to a short cane.

Aeschynanthus speciosus

Aeschynanthus

Evergreens of trailing or climbing habit and often living as air plants (epiphytes), the genus *Aeschynanthus* contains several excellent species for hanging baskets. Some have showy flowers, others decorative leaves as well. Among the most attractive are *A. speciosus*, which has the brightest flowers, and *A. radicans (lobbianus)* or lipstick plant. Before they open, the summer-borne flower buds are dusky-red tubes, with protruding folded crimson petals looking just like the top of a lipstick.

Position *Good light is needed, but protection from strong summer sunshine is essential. Medium night temperatures are adequate, around 55°F (13°C), but high humidity is necessary in summer.*

Water and food *Water regularly but moderately, allowing the potting mix to dry out partially between applications. Give liquid feed monthly, from spring through fall.*

Propagation *Stem tip cuttings about 4 in (10 cm) long root readily, especially in summer. Seed can be collected from the white berries that follow the flowers. Sow them in spring in a warm temperature, 66–70°F (18–21°C).*

A 10 in (25 cm) plastic-coated
wire hanging basket is an ideal
container for this plant. Line it
with moss and fill it with an
all-peat mix. One well grown plant
can be placed in the middle of the
basket, but for an instantaneous,
well-filled look, group three plants
together in the basket.

Aloe variegata

Aloe

Africa, Malagasy and Arabia are the home countries of the 275 *Aloe* species. They are succulent plants with narrow, fleshy leaves in rosettes and spikes of tubular flowers. Some species form ground-hugging rosettes, others develop into small trees. Most popular of all is *A. variegata* (partridge-breast aloe), which has a bonus of white-banded leaves. The pink to scarlet flowers open from late winter onward. *A. aristata* (torch plant) is very hardy and forms almost globular rosettes of whisker-pointed leaves. It bears orange-red flowers in early summer.

Position *Direct sunlight for part of each day is essential for regular flowering, though light shade during the hottest summer period is advisable. These plants will survive in cool temperatures. A minimum temperature of 40°F (5°C) is tolerated, though 45–50°F (7–10°C) is ideal.*

Water and food *Water freely during the late spring through early fall period and keep almost dry during the cool winter period. Apply liquid feed throughout the growing season at monthly intervals.*

Propagation *Remove offsets after flowering and place singly in small pots.*

Well grown plants of A. aristata *and* A. variegata *produce plenty of offsets. These arise just below ground level and should be removed by severing with a knife, ideally so that some roots are retained. Congested plants are best removed from their containers first.*

Insert each offset so that the leaf bases are just below the surface of the mix.

Anthurium Scherzeranum

Anthurium

Comparatively few of the 550 species in this genus have decorative flowers, though many have ornamental foliage. The showy part of each 'flower' is, in fact, a colored leaf known as a spathe, an organ typical of this family. The true flowers, minute and without petals, are crowded together to form the tail-like spike that arises from the spathe. *A. Scherzeranum* (flamingo flower) is the easiest species to keep in the home, but the taller, larger spathed *A. Andraeanum* is the more spectacular. All anthuriums prefer plenty of sphagnum moss or rough leaf mold added to the potting mix.

Position *Except during winter, anthuriums must be screened from direct sunlight. A north window is ideal, provided it gets plenty of light from the sky. Warm temperatures of around 60°F (16°C) are needed.*
Water and food *During early summer through late fall, keep the soil moist. For the rest of the year, give water only when the potting mix dries out.*
Propagation *Division of large plants in winter or spring is easy but care must be taken to damage the roots as little as possible.*

Divide only those plants with several crowns. Use a knife or bread saw to separate the roots of individual crowns, ensuring that each division has plenty of roots. Plant in a mixture of half moss, half potting mix.

Aphelandra squarrosa

Aphelandra

Only a few of the 200 known species in this tropical American genus are grown as house plants and only one widely so. They all have ornamental foliage and *A. squarrosa* (zebra plant) is spectacular in this respect. If it never produced a single flower, it would still be in demand. *A. aurantiaca roezlii* has less glossy leaves but silvery-white veining, which sets off the winter-blooming, bright orange-scarlet flowers. A third species, *A. Chamissoniana* (yellow spike), is a similar plant, with silvery-white variegated leaves and spikes of yellow flowers in winter.

Position *Bright light but not direct hot sunshine is necessary for the health of these plants, which like warm temperatures. A minimum of 60°F (16°C) is tolerated, but a little higher is better.*

Water and food *During the summer and fall growing season, give water regularly. For the rest of the year allow the potting mix to become almost dry between applications. Apply liquid feed at 10–14 day intervals throughout the growing period.*

Propagation *Stem cuttings, preferably of young shoots, root readily.*

Choose sturdy, healthy shoots for cuttings, ideally removing them before flower spikes can be seen at the tip.

Sever each shoot cleanly just below a node; after this remove the lowest one or two pairs of leaves.

Pot the cuttings, then cover each with a plastic bag to maintain humidity.

Aporocactus flagelliformis

Aporocactus

Unlike many cacti, the aporocacti not only have trailing or pendent stems but in their natural environment they grow epiphytically on trees and cliffs. *A. flagelliformis* is the common rattail cactus, with stems up to 6 ft (2 m) in length which bear a profusion of crimson-pink flowers. Almost as popular is the slightly more robust *A. Mallisonii*, with shorter, thicker stems and wider, redder flowers.

Position *To flower well these plants need bright light with at least three to four hours of direct sunshine daily. In winter they must be kept cool (a minimum temperature of 55–60°F, 13–16°C, must be maintained at night).*

Water and food *From late spring through late fall water regularly, but let the potting mix dry out partially between applications. For the rest of the year keep the plants almost dry.*

Propagation *Stem sections 4–5 in (10–13 cm) long, and ideally the tips, root readily. Allow them to dry for a few days before planting.*

Vigorous stem tips make the best cuttings. Remove them in summer with a sharp knife and, to protect fingers from the short sharp spines, hold the stems with a collar of folded paper. Plant cuttings after several days — singly or in groups.

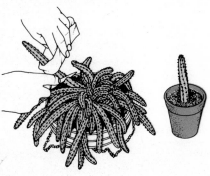

Begonia × tuberhybrida

Begonia

This huge genus of some 1,000 species has much to offer the lover of house plants. Almost all have curiously lopsided, often ear-shaped leaves, which in some cases are attractively variegated. For impact of flowers, the race of hybrids known as *B. × tuberhybrida* are unsurpassed. These are the familiar hybrid tuberous begonias. The huge, double-flowered, erect stemmed types are classified as Camellia-flowered and make good pot plants. The smaller bloomed, slender stemmed kinds are known as Pendula-flowered and make good hanging basket subjects.

Position *Bright light is necessary but shade from hot summer sunshine is important. They must have warm temperatures, a minimum of 60°F (16°C).*
Water and food *When tubers are newly potted or started in trays of peat in early spring, water them sparingly. As growth develops, more water is necessary and the potting mix must be kept damp. The plants must be dried off in fall. During active growth, feed at two-weekly intervals.*
Propagation *Cut tubers into sections, each with a shoot. Alternatively, take stem cuttings, each ideally attached to a sliver of tuber.*

Before dividing the tubers, they must first be started into growth in trays of moist peat in warmth. When shoots are visible, slice the tubers with a sharp knife into two or more sections, each with one shoot. Immediately pot the sections singly.

Billbergia nutans

Billbergia

The majority of the species in this New World genus are air plants (epiphytes). *B. nutans* (queen's tears or friendship plant) from Brazil is best known, with its clumps of dark green, tubular-based rosettes and slender, flowering stalks with rose-red bracts. Less familiar is *B. decora*, which has grayish-white banded leaves and larger pink bracts on the flowering stalk. More decorative than either is the plant produced by mating these two species, *B. × Windii*, which is as tough as *B. nutans* but has grayish leaves and blue tipped, pink bracts.

Position *Bright light is needed for good flowering, ideally with a few hours direct sunshine each day. These plants tolerate cool night temperatures down to 40°F (5°C).*
Water and food *Water regularly but allow the potting mix to dry out partially between applications. Feed established plants monthly.*
Propagation *Divide congested plants into small clumps. Alternatively, remove well-rooted offsets from the bases of rosettes that have finished flowering.*

The easiest way to propagate a billbergia is to divide it. This is best done after flowering. Remove the plant from its container and shake some of the potting mix off or tease it away with a small fork. Then push a sharp knife into the center of the plant to sever the roots and pull the two halves apart.

Bougainvillea × Buttiana

Bougainvillea

Although most spectacular as large plants trained in the roof of a greenhouse, bougainvilleas make very satisfactory pot specimens trained as bushes.

Position *Bright light and as much direct sunshine as possible is essential for these plants. They will only tolerate winter temperatures down to about 45–50°F (7–10°C) but 55°F (13°C) is preferred.*

Water and food *Water regularly during the growing season but allow the surface of the potting mix to dry out between applications. Keep almost dry in winter. Apply liquid feed at two-weekly intervals during the growing season.*

Propagation *Take semi-hardwood cuttings in spring or summer, or hardwood cuttings in late winter. Keep both warm at about 70°F (21°C).*

To create a bush plant that requires no support, trim a rooted cutting to about 6 in (15 cm), severing just above a leaf.

When the shoots that develop have three or four leaves, pinch out the tips to promote even more shoots.

As soon as each of the new crop of shoots has three leaves, pinch out the stem tips for the last time.

Browallia speciosa major

Browallia

Two of the six species in this genus are regularly grown in green-houses and make showy, short-term pot plants. Both are technically shrubby perennials but are best treated as annuals. *B. speciosa major* is the best known and forms a bushy plant up to 3 ft (90 cm) or more, studded with rich purple-blue flowers 1½ in (4 cm) wide. *B. viscosa* is 1–1½ ft (30–45 cm) tall and has smaller leaves and flowers. Really compact is *B.v.* 'Sapphire', only 6–10 in (15–25 cm) tall and free-flowering. Both normally flower from summer through late fall. However, where there is good light it is possible to sow seeds in early fall to bring on plants that will flower in winter.

Position *Bright light is necessary, with several hours of direct sunshine each day. A medium temperature, minimum 55°F (13°C), is essential, but ideally a little higher for free-flowering.*
Water and food *Water regularly but moderately, making sure that the potting mix does not stay wet for long periods. Apply liquid feed at two-weekly intervals once the plants have been established in their final pots for six weeks.*
Propagation *Sow seed in early spring in a warm temperature of about 65°F (18°C).*

Young plants of B. speciosa tend to be sparsely branched unless they are stopped. Pinch out or stop the first branches when they reach 4–6 in (10–15 cm). For a really bushy plant, pinch out the shoots that then arise once they reach this length.

Brunfelsia australis

Brunfelsia

The vernacular name Yesterday-today-and-tomorrow is most apt for the evergreen shrub *B. australis*. The long-tubed, 2 in (5 cm) wide flowers open blue-purple and over a period of two to three days age to lavender-blue, then almost white. The best form is *B.c.* 'Macrantha' with larger, finer flowers than the species plant; *B.c.* 'Floribunda' is a free-flowering dwarf.

Position *To flower well, a site in bright light is necessary with at least two or three hours of direct sunshine each day, except in high summer. During the early part of winter a six-week rest at a medium temperature (about 50–55 °F, 10–13 °C) is required to stimulate free flowering.*

Water and food *Water regularly during the growing season, but allow the surface of the potting mix to dry between applications. Keep on the dry side during its winter rest period. Apply liquid feed to established specimens at two-weekly intervals during the summer.*

Propagation *Take cuttings in spring, ideally of shoot tips about 3½ in (9 cm) long. Keep them in a warm temperature of about 70°F (21°C).*

Remove dead or faded flowers regularly to keep the plant looking neat and fresh. This procedure also helps to encourage the production of further blossom.

Calceolaria crenatiflora

Calceolaria

Among the 300 species in this genus are annuals, biennials, perennials and shrubs, some tender but others hardy. Best known among those used as pot plants is the hybrid group *C. crenatiflora* (often called *C. × herbeohybrida*). The huge, pouch-like flowers are borne in clusters in spring and can be shades of red, yellow or orange, often spotted with a contrasting color. They are biennials and grow to about 1½ ft (45 cm) tall, though dwarf types that grow to only half this are available.

Position *Bright light is necessary, with direct sunshine from late fall through early spring. A cool night temperature of 45–50°F (7–10°C) and by day a warm temperature, maximum 65°F (18°C), is ideal.*

Water and food *Water regularly and carefully, making sure not to splash water on the flowers or making the potting mix too moist. Apply liquid feed at 10–14 day intervals, from six weeks after the final potting.*

Propagation *Seeds are the only means of propagation. They must be sown in summer and kept at a cool temperature.*

Potting-on is very important when vigorous, fast growing plants such as calceolaria have been raised from seed. This is best done as soon as the leaves overlap the sides of the pot and roots appear at the drainage holes (left). Failure to pot-on then will mean smaller plants and fewer flowers. Repot the small plant in a container that gives about an inch (2.5 cm) of space all round the root ball (right).

Campanula isophylla

Campanula

Most of the 300 bellflowers are hardy herbaceous perennials, the many dwarf varieties being popular for rock gardens. Only one, *C. isophylla*, is grown as an indoor plant and even this is almost hardy. Sometimes called Italian bellflower or falling stars, *C. isophylla* has a trailing habit that suits it admirably for a hanging basket. It is a variable plant. The common form has bright green, smooth leaves and lilac-blue flowers. *C.i.* 'Alba' has pure white blooms and *C.i.* 'Mayi' somewhat grayish, hairy, white variegated foliage and the normal lilac-blue flowers. All bloom from late summer through early winter.

Position *Bright light is essential, ideally with a few hours of direct sunlight each day except in high summer. During the winter, a cool rest period at less than 50°F (10°C) is necessary.*

Water and food *During the growing season, water regularly but not excessively. Keep almost dry in winter. Apply liquid feed once a month from late spring through early fall.*

Propagation *The easiest method is by division in late winter. Alternatively, take cuttings of young shoots in early spring.*

Large specimens of C. isophylla *can be divided to create more plants. Three- to four-year-old plants are best. Turn them out of their pots or hanging baskets and separate the clumps that will have formed with two hand forks. Plant each clump in a separate pot.*

Catharanthus roseus

Catharanthus

Widely grown outdoors where summers are hot and humid, the rose or Madagascar (Malagasy) periwinkle, *C. roseus*, makes a showy pot plant in cooler climates. Formerly known as *Vinca rosea* and still often found under this name, it is an evergreen shrubby plant that grows to 2 ft (60 cm), though usually less. The spring- to fall-borne flowers come in shades of pink to white.

Position *Bright light is essential, with as much direct sunshine as possible. Without this, the plants become leggy and flower poorly. A medium temperature, 55–60°F (13–16°C), is necessary.*

Water and food *Water regularly but allow the surface of the potting mix to dry between applications. Apply liquid feed at two-weekly intervals to well established specimens.*

Propagation *A sowing of seed in a warm temperature, about 65°F (18°C), in early spring will flower around mid-summer. Alternatively, take stem tip cuttings in spring or summer and keep them at the same temperature.*

Sow seeds thinly in seed-sowing mix, ideally spacing them out with fingers or a pair of tweezers so that they are ½ in (1 cm) apart (right). Cover the seed shallowly with a layer of the seed-sowing mix, then water and place the container in a plastic bag or a propagating case (far right).

Cineraria × hybridus

Cineraria

The daisy-flowered pot plant *C. × hybridus* is sometimes described more correctly as *Senecio × hybridus*. It is also often referred to as *Senecio cruentus*, though this name correctly applies to one of its Canary Island parents. It is a variable hybrid, the flowers coming in shades of pink, red, mauve, purple, lavender and white, often strikingly bicolored. Different forms grow to different heights. *C. multiflora nana* has a compact habit to 1 ft (30 cm); *C. multiflora* is similar but grows to about 1½ ft (45 cm), while *C. stellata* is looser and attains 2–2½ ft (60–75 cm) in height. All need cool growing conditions.

Position *These plants need moderately bright light but not direct sunshine, except in winter. A cool night temperature, about 45–50°F (7–10°C), is required, with an ideal warm maximum of about 65°F (18°C) by day.*
Water and food *Watering must be carried out regularly but with care, for over-wet potting mix soon leads to root rot. Apply liquid feed at two weekly intervals, once the plants have been in their final pots for six weeks.*
Propagation *Seed is the usual method. A spring sowing will bloom the following winter, a summer sowing in the following spring.*

Early pricking out is important for cineraria seedlings. To delay will mean tangled roots and slowed growth. When the first true leaf is clearly visible on each seedling, gently dig up the tiny plants and plant each in its own pot of potting mix.

Citrus mitis

Citrus

This genus embraces such familiar citrus fruits as orange, lemon, tangerine and grapefruit. All are evergreen shrubs or small trees with fragrant white flowers. Grown from pips, they make handsome foliage plants but take many years to flower and fruit. The best *Citrus* to grow as a house plant is *C. mitis*, the calamondin or Panama orange.

Position *Bright light with several hours of sunshine daily is needed for a good showing of flowers and fruits. The plants benefit from standing outside in summer. In winter, a medium temperature, minimum 50°F (10°C), is adequate but a little higher is preferable.*

Water and food *Water regularly but moderately and provide humidity during the growing season. In winter, allow the potting mix to dry out partially between waterings. Feed twice weekly from late spring through early fall.*

Propagation *Take semi-hardwood cuttings with a heel in late summer. Keep them in a warm temperature, 65–70°F (18–21°C).*

Whether grown from pips or cuttings, all the best known species of **Citrus**, *particularly orange, lemon and grapefruit, tend to grow straight up with few side branches. To create more shapely, bushy plants, pinch or cut out the growing tips once branches reach 4–6 in (10–15 cm) in length.*

Clerodendrum Thomsoniae

Clerodendrum

No less than 400 species of trees, shrubs and climbers form this genus, but only one has become a popular house plant. This is *C. Thomsoniae*, popularly known as the bleeding-glory-vine, from West Africa. Although not pretty, this vernacular name is apt, for the white, heart-shaped flower buds split to disclose red petals. It is an evergreen climber of some vigor, but can be kept to 6 ft (2 cm) or less by regular pinching out of growing tips.

Position *Bright light is necessary but direct sunshine must be screened in summer. Provide humidity, especially during the growing season. These plants need to rest in a medium temperature, minimum 55°F (13°C), for six to eight weeks in winter to stimulate flowering.*

Water and food *During the growing season water freely, but avoid over-wet potting mix. Give established plants liquid feed at two weekly intervals from late spring through fall.*

Propagation *Cuttings are easiest if taken in late spring or summer and given a warm temperature, minimum 70°F (21°C). Layering in spring is also possible.*

A variety of supports can be made or purchased for this climbing plant. The most effective is a fan-shaped structure about 2 ft (60 cm) tall, made of canes bound together. The stems will naturally twine straight up the canes. When they get to the top, pinch out the growing tips. Side shoots will develop; tie them horizontally along the cross pieces.

Clivia miniata

Clivia

A ll three species of *Clivia* are decorative, but *C. miniata* is outstand-ing in its showiness and tolerance of poor conditions. For the best effect, pot-on plants until they have at least eight to ten of their big, leek-like, dark green shoots. Such plants can produce up to six flower heads each year. Clivias are sometimes referred to as Kaffir lilies from their South African homeland. This name, however, can lead to confu-sion, since another plant, *Schizostylis coccinea*, is also called Kaffir lily.

Position *Bright light encourages flowering, but direct sunshine is not essential, although it can be beneficial in fall through winter. A winter rest in a cool temperature (less than 50°F, 10°C) is necessary.*

Water and food *During the main summer growing season keep the potting mix regularly moist. At other times allow the potting mix partially to dry out between waterings. Apply liquid feed at three to four weekly intervals from late spring through late summer.*

Propagation *Congested plants can be divided after flowering. Alternatively, separate three to four well-rooted offsets from the parent at the same time of year.*

Clivias like to be left undisturbed to form free-flowering clumps and only when large and congested should they be divided. Offsets, however, can be taken from a clump without too much disturbance. Turn the plant out of its container and sever a rooted shoot with a knife, carefully teasing and pulling it away from the parent. Pot the offset at once.

Columnea microphylla

Columnea

Most of the 200 species in this tropical American genus are air plants (epiphytes), that in their natural habitat perch on and cascade from mossy branches. All are evergreen and bear tubular flowers with wide, gaping mouths in shades of red, orange, pink or yellow. The trailing species, *C. microphylla*, *C. gloriosa*, and such hybrids as *C.g.* 'Superba', make the most spectacular hanging basket specimens in the home. *C. linearis* is a bushy plant that grows to 1½ ft (45 cm) tall with pink flowers; the hybrid *C.* 'Chanticleer' is more compact.

Position *Bright light but not direct sunshine is necessary for free-flowering, and a warm winter temperature, around 60°F (16°C) or above. Kept almost dry, they will survive at temperatures down to 50°F (10°C).*

Water and food *Water regularly but allow the potting mix almost to dry out between applications. Provide humidity and liquid feed every two weeks.*

Propagation *Stem cuttings taken in summer root easily in a warm temperature, minimum 65–70°F (18–21°C).*

Columneas are ideal hanging-basket plants. A plastic-coated wire mesh basket is best, ideally 10 in (25 cm) wide. Thickly line the basket with moss or plastic sheeting in which drainage holes have been made, then fill it with an all-peat potting mix. A single, well grown plant can be placed in the middle and lightly firmed or, for a more instantly decorative effect, insert three to five rooted cuttings around the edge of the basket.

Crossandra infundibuliformis

Crossandra

Although two or three species in this 50-strong genus are sometimes grown as house plants, only one is commonly seen. This is *C. infundibuliformis*, formerly known, and still sometimes referred to, as *C. undulifolia*. It has bright, salmon red flowers and although potentially a shrub to at least 3 ft (90 cm) tall, it is best kept to half this by pruning in spring.

Position *Bright light is required but direct sunshine must be screened in summer. A warm temperature is essential and must not fall below 60°F (16°C), but 65°F (18°C) is ideal.*

Water and food *During the growing season, water regularly but never allow the potting mix to stay permanently wet. Provide humidity. Feed established plants at two weekly intervals from spring through fall.*

Propagation *Take cuttings, using non-flowering shoots from cut-back plants, in late spring. Keep them in a warm temperature, minimum 70°F (21°C).*

Young plants must be potted-on regularly. First turn the plant upside down across the hand and then rap the pot rim down on a hard surface.

Prepare a larger pot with a layer of potting mix in the bottom. Place the root ball of the plant in the new pot.

Holding the plant in position, carefully pour new potting mix into the space between root ball and pot and gently firm it.

Cuphea ignea

Cuphea

Comparatively few of the 250 species in this genus are cultivated and even fewer are used as house plants. They are highly distinctive, with a long season of uniquely slender, tubular flowers. *C. ignea* is still often found under its earlier name, *C. platycentra*. Commonly known as cigar flower, it is a bushy, almost shrubby perennial to 1 ft (30 cm) or so in height. Equally as tall or more so, but more densely bushy and with wiry stems and tiny leaves, is *C. hyssopifolia*, sometimes aptly named false heather. It bears rose-purple flowers in summer and fall.

Position *Bright light is necessary with at least a few hours of direct sunshine daily. A rest period in a medium temperature, minimum 50°F (10°C), is vital during the winter.*

Water and food *Water regularly during the growing season but sparingly in winter. Apply liquid feed to established plants from spring through fall at about two-weekly intervals.*

Propagation *Cuttings of non-flowering shoots usually root readily in late summer or early fall. Seeds may be sown in spring. Both methods require a warm temperature of about 65–70°F (18–21°C).*

Select non-flowering shoots to use as cuttings. Trim cuttings of C. ignea *to about 2½ in (6 cm) in length, those of* C. hyssopifolia *to about 2 in (5 cm). If flower buds are present in the tips, pinch them out. Space the cuttings ¾–1 in (2–2.5 cm) apart, then enclose the pot in a plastic bag.*

Cyclamen persicum

Cyclamen

The so-called Persian or florists' cyclamen, *C. persicum*, is one of the most popular of all flowering pot plants. It is extremely variable in flower, leaf size and color. Cultivated varieties have flowers of pink to crimson-purple and white, and all shades in between. Plants will survive for many years if they are dried off in late spring, rested through the summer months and re-potted and watered to start them into growth in late summer.

Position *Moderately bright light is necessary, with shading from direct sunshine from late spring through fall. A medium temperature, minimum 45–50°F (7–10°C) and a maximum of 65°F (18°C), is the ideal.*
Water and food *Water moderately, allowing the potting mix to dry out partially between applications and avoiding wetting the top of the corm. Apply liquid feed at two-weekly intervals to plants established in their final pots.*
Propagation *If large plants are required, sow seed in fall; if small plants are preferred, sow in spring. Keep seedlings at a medium temperature 55–60°F (13–16°C).*

Although unsuited to the high temperatures of centrally heated homes, cyclamen will last longer if given humid conditions. Stand the plants on trays of gravel or small pebbles flooded with water. The water will need topping up regularly, but it must not rise above the surface of the pebbles or it will soak the root ball.

Cytisus × spachianus

Cytisus

Nurserymen usually, but wrongly, call this attractive Canary Islands broom *C. canariensis*, *C. racemosus* or *Genista fragrans*. Its correct name is *C. × spachianus*. Although a shrub capable of attaining 15 ft (5 m) in height, it flowers when very young and no more that 1 ft (30 cm) tall. Of elegant arching growth, the slim stem bears distinctly stalked, trifoliate leaves. Profusely carried short spikes of fragrant, rich yellow pea flowers open in winter and spring.

Position *Bright light is necessary, ideally with direct sun as well. Half-day shade is tolerated but flowering may be less profuse.*

Water and food *Give water regularly to maintain a moist, but not wet, potting mix. Apply liquid feed at two-weekly intervals to well established plants. For winter flowering, a medium temperature, minimum 45–50°F (7–10°C), must be maintained.*

Propagation *Take semi-hardwood cuttings in late summer.*

Cuttings of this decorative plant should be of lateral shoots starting to get woody at the base. Pull these off carefully by grasping the base of the shoot with thumb and forefinger and pulling backward and downward.

The basal 'tail' of parent stem must be cut off and the tip removed, so that the completed cutting is about 2½–3 in (6–7.5 cm) long. After dipping the stems in rooting powder, space the cuttings 1 in (2.5 cm) apart, then enclose them in a propagator or plastic bag.

Dipladenia (Mandevilla) Sanderi

Dipladenia

Although the name *Dipladenia* is still used among gardeners, botanically this genus is now classified under *Mandevilla*. All species are climbing plants, some exceedingly showy. The most widely grown as a pot plant is *M. Sanderi* from Brazil. It can reach 10–15 ft (3–5 m) in a tub, but if pruned hard in late winter, cutting away most of the previous year's lateral stems, it can be trained on a support and kept to 3 ft (90 cm) tall. Alternatively, it can be grown as a small, loose bush by pinching out side shoots and confining in a 6 in (15 cm) pot.

Position *Bright light is necessary but direct sunshine is not essential. This plant must rest during the winter months so keep in a medium temperature, minimum 55°F (13°C), during this period.*
Water and food *During the growing season the potting mix must be kept moist but not wet. Water less during the rest period. Apply liquid feed to established plants at two-weekly intervals during the growing period.*
Propagation *Take cuttings of young shoots or leaf bud cuttings in spring and keep them in a warm temperature, not less than 75°F (24°C). It is also possible to layer these plants.*

Although dipladenias can be propagated by ordinary stem cuttings, leaf bud cuttings root more readily. These, which consist of a pair of leaves and a 1–1½ in (2.5–4 cm) length of parent stem, are best cut away from newly mature branches.

It is best to split the stem lengthwise into two, leaving one leaf attached to each piece. Dust these single leaved cuttings with a rooting powder and insert obliquely into a small pot of potting mix.

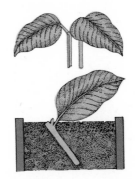

Echeveria Derenbergii

Echeveria

This popular genus of succulents provides many decorative and long-suffering house plants. There are two broad groups, those that form houseleek-like rosettes and those that develop into small, soft stemmed shrubs. *E. Derenbergii* produces compact rosettes of blue-green, red-tipped leaves and short stems with orange-red flowers. It is sometimes called baby echeveria or painted-lady. *E. harmsii* belongs to the shrubby group and can attain 1 ft (30 cm) in height. It has the largest flowers among the cultivated species, up to 1¼ in (3 cm) in length. They appear in spring and summer.

Position *As much direct sunlight as possible is essential to maintain sturdy plants that flower well. Allow a rest period at a medium temperature, minimum 50°F (10°C), in winter.*

Water and food *Water regularly during the growing season but allow the potting mix almost to dry out between applications. In winter, water only sufficiently to prevent leaves becoming limp. Liquid feed at monthly intervals is beneficial during the growing period.*

Propagation *Take cuttings of shrubby species and remove offsets from rosette types in spring. Both kinds can also be increased by leaf cuttings.*

Rosette-forming echeverias are prone to attack by red spider mites and mealy bugs. They are difficult to eradicate by spraying with insecticide since they hide in the overlapping leaves. The most efficient method of applying insecticide, therefore, is to use a small paintbrush, working the insecticide well into the leaf bases.

Epiphyllum hybrid

Epiphyllum

The plants popularly grown as epiphyllums are mostly hybrids with other cactus genera, notably *Heliocereus* and *Selenicereus*. They are often known as orchid cacti, because of their large, pink, red, purple, yellow or white blooms carried on sparse, leaf-like stems. Their wild progenitors are air plants (epiphytes), which perch on the branches of tropical forest trees in South America. In the home these plants need shade and humidity and thrive in small pots of humus-rich soil.

Position *These plants need only moderate light and must be screened from direct sunshine. Medium temperatures, 50–60°F (10–16°C), are ideal.*

Water and food *Water regularly but allow the potting mix to dry out between applications. If kept below the recommended temperature, very little water is required in winter. Liquid feed is beneficial at two- to three-weekly intervals in the summer months.*

Propagation *Cuttings root with ease in late spring and early summer. Cut a mature stem into 5–6 in (13–15 cm) sections.*

Owing to their complicated hybrid ancestry, epiphyllums show great variability. Most of the cultivars have flattened stems which resemble leaves, but vary in the amount of notching or toothing on the margins (right). Some cultivars have stems that are triangular in cross section, the edges of which may or may not be winged.

Episcia reptans

Episcia

This genus of trailing evergreen perennials from central and southern America provides attractive foliage and flowers. The plants form clumps of oval leaves, often with a metallic luster, from which emerge stolons, fast-growing stems with further tufts of leaves at intervals. The tubular flowers may be white, lavender or red. All can be grown as smallish pot plants by pinching out the stolons. However, they are much more effective when grown naturally in hanging baskets. Species to look for are *E. cupreata* and *E. reptans*, both with rich, red flowers, and *E. dianthiflora*, which has large, fringed white flowers.

Position *Keep these plants in moderately bright light with, ideally, a few hours of direct sunshine each day from mid-fall through mid-spring. They need a warm temperature around 65°F (18°C).*
Water and food *Give enough water to keep the potting mix moist but not wet, and liquid feed at two-weekly intervals from spring through fall.*
Propagation *The easiest method is layering the stolons. Alternatively, sever the rosette-like, leafy tufts and treat them as cuttings.*

The trailing habit of episcias can look attractive in a hanging basket but can become a disadvantage with a pot-grown plant, since the long stems look untidy. Remove the stolons regularly from pot plants (right). This will also encourage the growth of plenty of flowers.

Euphorbia pulcherrima

Euphorbia

This vast genus of 2,000 species contains annuals, perennials, shrubs and small trees, both hardy and tender. It also embraces a wide range of succulent plants. The best known houseplant species is *E. pulcherrima*, more familiarly called poinsettia, which is at its best around Christmas time. The showy part of the flower clusters is not provided by flowers but by colored leaves known as bracts.

Position *Bright light is essential, with several hours of direct sunshine each day, except in the hottest summer period. A warm temperature, minimum 60°F (16°C), is vital for actively growing plants but allow the plants to rest after flowering in medium temperatures down to 50°F (10°C).*

Water and food *Water regularly during the growing season, but allow the potting mix almost to dry out between applications during the winter rest period. Apply liquid feed to established plants at two-weekly intervals during the summer and fall.*

Propagation *Take stem cuttings of young shoots from cut-back plants in late spring. The white sap must be washed off before the cutting is dipped in a rooting powder prior to planting. Keep in a warm temperature, about 70°F (21°C).*

Plants resting after flowering will lose most of their leaves, though some of the upper ones and withered flower clusters may remain. Just before the first watering in spring, cut back all the top growth to about 4 in (10 cm). Water copiously the first time, then keep the plant warm to encourage vigorous growth. For two months in fall give at least 14 hours per day of total darkness once new growth has started, to encourage flowers.

Exacum affine

Exacum

The species *E. affine* is the only one of this genus of 30 species to be used as a house plant. A native of the island of Socotra, it is sometimes called German or Persian violet. Despite these vernacular names and its family classification, it is neither like a violet nor a gentian. It is a bushy plant with small, almost fleshy leaves and bears a succession of wide open, bluish-purple flowers from spring through fall. Although described as an annual, it often lives for up to two years.

Position *Bright light is necessary but it must be screened from direct sunshine from late spring through fall. A medium temperature, not less than 55°F (13°C), is essential.*

Water and food *Water regularly, keeping the potting mix moist but do not allow it to remain wet for long periods. Apply liquid feed at two-weekly intervals, from about six weeks after the final potting.*

Propagation *Sow seed in early spring in a warm temperature, about 65°F (18°C). A succession of sowings in summer through fall will provide flowering plants throughout the year.*

As with so many flowering pot plants, the removal of faded flowers greatly improves their overall appearance. Picking off faded flowers also prevents the formation of seed and encourages the plants to produce more blooms. However, if seed is required for propagation, at least some of the flowers must be left so that pods can form.

Fuchsia hybrid

Fuchsia

The fact that there are societies devoted to this genus is evidence of its great popularity. About 100 species and thousands of hybrids and cultivated varieties are known. All are shrubs or small trees. Those popular as pot plants are hybrids, available with both double and single flowers in shades of red, pink, purple and white. They are easily grown and respond to a variety of methods of training, from bushes to pyramids and standards. They must not, however, be kept too hot and they need plenty of humidity to thrive and flower well.

Position *Bright light is essential with several hours of direct sunshine daily, except during the hottest summer period. Warm temperatures, maximum 70°F (21°C), in summer are best, though short periods above this are tolerated. Fuchsias need a winter rest in cool temperatures of less than 50°F (10°C).*

Water and food *The potting mix must be kept moist but never allowed to stay too wet. During the winter rest period water only sparingly. Humidity is vital in summer. Feed at seven to 10 day intervals during the growing season.*

Propagation *Cuttings can be taken in late summer or early spring. Young shoot tips about 2 in (5 cm) long root quickly and grow rapidly.*

Most potted fuchsias are grown as bushes. To keep them shapely and compact, pinch out the tips of new shoots on rooted cuttings when the shoots reach 4–6 in (10–15 cm). Subsequent shoots must also be pinched out.

Gardenia jasminoides

Gardenia

Although gardenias are used as nosegays at weddings and to scent perfume, the plant is still little known, probably because it has an unfair reputation for being difficult to grow. An evergreen shrub, *G. jasminoides*, comes from southern China. It is nearly always found in its double-flowered form, *G.j.* 'Fortuniana', which flowers in summer, or the form brought into flower in winter by growers, *G.j.* 'Veitchii'. Although potentially a flowering shrub reaching 6 ft (2 m) in height, it responds well to pot culture and can easily be kept small by pinching out the growing tips.

Position *Bright light is necessary for flowering but direct sunlight must be screened from mid-spring through fall. Plants thrive in warm temperatures, 60–70°F (16–21°C), for most of the year. However, during the period when buds are forming a steady temperature of 62–63°F (17°C) must be maintained to prevent buds falling off.*

Water and food *Water regularly but allow the top of the potting mix to dry out between applications. In winter, reduce the amounts of water to slow down growth. Give established plants liquid feed every two weeks during the summer.*

Propagation *Cuttings of young shoots in spring usually root in a warm temperature, 60–70°F (16–21°C).*

As gardenias age, plants tend to become leggy and untidy. This can be prevented by regularly cutting out the tips of shoots that have finished flowering, thinning twiggy, non-blooming growth and tipping any strong stems that have grown too big.

Gesneria (Sinningia) cardinalis

Gesneria

Provided warmth and humidity are adequate, several gesnerias make cheerful and distinctive house plants. One of the best is *G. cardinalis* (correctly, part of the genus *Sinningia*), a native of Brazil. Each spring it sends up stems to 1 ft (30 cm), clad with dark-veined, large, oval, bright green leaves. The scarlet flowers are 2–3 in (5–7.5 cm) long and open in summer. The plant dies back to a woody corm in the fall. Rather different is the dwarf *G. cuneifolia*, which is evergreen and carries bright red blooms.

Position *Bright light is required with, ideally, several hours of direct sunshine each day. Keep gesnerias in a warm temperature of 60°F (16°C) or above. The dormant corms of* G. cardinalis *must be stored in a medium temperature, 50–60°F (10–16°C).*
Water and food *Keep the soil just moist. Allow* G. cardinalis *to dry off in fall. In spring, water the corms sparingly and gradually increase amounts. Feed established plants at two-week intervals until flowering ceases.*
Propagation G. cardinalis *can be propagated by cutting up the corm as it starts into growth. Alternatively, take basal shoots as cuttings. Increase* G. cuneifolia *from suckers.*

The corms of G. cardinalis *can be cut up as a means of increase. First, start them into growth in containers of moist peat. Keep at a warm temperature. As soon as shoots are clearly visible, slice the corms into sections, ensuring that each section has a shoot. Plant the sections and treat them as whole corms.*

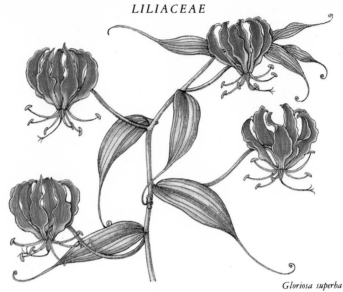

Gloriosa superba

Gloriosa

The climbing Gloriosa lilies from Africa and Asia have been largely overlooked as house plants until recent years. Their 4–6 ft (1.2–2 m) stems need a large window and a support of canes, but apart from this they are easy to grow and are spectacular. The slender stems are clad with bright green leaves that taper to slender points with hooked tips. It is best to tie the stems to their supports. *G. Rothschildiana* and *G. superba* are sometimes confused, but the latter has strongly waved, crimped petals.

Position *Bright light is best, with several hours of direct sunshine each day. Medium temperatures suit these plants. Store dormant tubers at a cool temperature, around 50°F (10°C).*

Water and food *When tubers are potted in spring, water sparingly, but as the plants grow keep the potting mix moist but not wet. Liquid feed twice a month once the plants are 1–1½ ft (30–45 cm) tall. Allow the tubers to dry off thoroughly in fall.*

Propagation *The natural increase of the tubers each year makes propagation an automatic process.*

Flowering-sized gloriosa lily tubers are curiously forked and about 4 in (10 cm) long with growing points at both tips.

Before potting, it is best to break the forked tubers into two. Snap them apart at the point of the 'V'. Fill a pot half full with potting mix and place the half tubers in a ring, nose to tail.

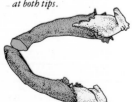

Haemanthus albiflos

Haemanthus

The name of this genus of bulbous plants is Greek for blood flower and the best known common name is blood lily. Fireball lily is another name for the species which have globular flower heads. Although most of the 60 species have red or pink flowers, the best known house plant, *H. albiflos*, has white flowers. Unlike other species, it is evergreen and will thrive without direct sunshine. *H. Katharinae* bears spectacular globular heads of red flowers on 1 ft (30 cm) tall stems in summer. It must be dried off in winter, when it will lose its handsome large leaves.

Position H. albiflos *needs bright light;* H. katharinae *must have a few hours of direct sunshine each day. Medium temperatures, around 50–60°F (10–16°C), are adequate. Store dormant bulbs at a similar temperature.*
Water and food *Water regularly but allow the potting mix almost to dry out between applications.* H. katharinae *appreciates humidity when in full growth but must be kept dry in winter. Apply liquid feed twice a month during the growing season. Re-pot every third year.*
Propagation *Separate offsets when plants are re-potted. Grow them on individually in small pots.*

All the haemanthuses eventually form offsets, though it may be several years before this happens. Offsets are big enough to be removed when they come away from the parent with only gentle finger pressure. Separate them during the dormant season, then pot each in a small pot of potting mix and treat as an adult bulb.

Hibiscus rosa-sinensis

Hibiscus

Large and colorful, the wide, funnel-shaped blossoms of hibiscuses are very much the symbols of tropical luxuriance. Most are hybrids with flowers in shades of red, pink, yellow or white; some are bicolored.

Position *Bright light is essential, with several hours of direct sunshine daily. This plant thrives in medium or warm temperatures but it must be given a cool winter rest at a medium temperature of about 55°F (13°C).*

Water and food *Water regularly during the growing season but avoid over-wet conditions. In winter, water more sparingly. Apply liquid feed at two-weekly intervals from late spring through early fall.*

Propagation *Take young shoot or semi-hardwood cuttings from spring through late summer. Keep them in a warm temperature, about 70°F (21°C).*

This shrubby plant makes many side shoots which are ideal for propagation purposes. Even if more plants are not wanted, it is wise to remove unwanted shoots and to cut back long branches in spring.

To propagate new plants, take young shoots with a heel attached from the main plant during the spring.

Plant each shoot in damp potting mix and then enclose the potted cutting in a plastic bag. Put it in bright light, only removing it from the bag once the roots have begun to grow.

Hippeastrum hybrid

Hippeastrum

Largest blossomed of all the flowering plants, the hippeastrum, or amaryllis as it is generally known, provides tropical splendor on the window-ledge for the modest purchase price of a bulb. In recent years, Dutch growers have mass produced these bulbs and they are now available almost everywhere. The most readily available bulbs are of hybrid origin and produce flowers in late winter or spring in shades of pink, red, orange or white, and are sometimes bicolored.

Position *Bright light is necessary, with a few hours of direct sunshine each day during the growing season. Medium temperatures, 50–60°F (10–16°C), are best since higher temperatures, though tolerated, shorten the life of the flowers.*
Water and food *Bulbs are usually planted in early summer. Water newly potted bulbs sparingly but, as flower buds and foliage grows, give more — enough to keep the potting mix moist but never wet. Give liquid feed at two-weekly intervals during the summer months.*
Propagation *Detach offsets at re-potting time.*

Hippeastrum growth follows a regular yearly cycle. Dry bulbs are acquired during the dormant winter period. Soaking the base of the bulb before planting will encourage root growth. The flower bud emerges in late winter or early spring, followed by tall leaves that remain throughout the summer. Then the bulb must be allowed to dry.

Hoya carnosa

Hoya

Most of the 200 species in this South-East Asian and Pacific islands' genus are climbers, but some are more shrubby and live as air plants (epiphytes) on the branches of trees. Best known is the wax plant, *H. carnosa*. It can grow 12–18 ft (4–6 m) in a tub but is easily kept to a more manageable height in a small pot. Nevertheless, a large plant trained on a frame can present an eye-catching sight when in full bloom during the summer. *H. bella* is a small, neat epiphyte with pendent branches and looks splendid in a hanging basket.

Position *Bright light is necessary for free-flowering and, except during the hottest months, a few hours daily of direct sunshine are desirable. Medium temperatures with a minimum of 50–55°F (10–13°C) are most suitable.*

Water and food *Water in moderation, allowing the potting mix almost to dry out between applications. Liquid feed at two to three weekly intervals is beneficial during the growing season.*

Propagation *Stem cuttings root readily in summer, or stems can be layered from spring through fall.*

A simple inverted 'U' or hoop provides an effective support for H. carnosa. *The stems must be tied to their supports initially, but will soon twine upwards. When stems reach the top of the support, tie them to form a complete circle.*

Hyacinthus orientalis

Hyacinthus

The common or Dutch hyacinth, *H. orientalis*, has long been popular for winter and spring color in the home. It is hardy and therefore only a short term house plant. Bulbs must be potted in the fall, setting them with their necks just above the surface of the potting mix, and kept as cool as possible, at least under 50°F (10°C) by night. This aids the growth of a strong root system. After flowering, bulbs can be planted in the garden.

Position *Bright light is necessary to keep the flower spikes sturdy and a few hours of direct sunshine daily are beneficial. Cool to medium temperatures are essential for a long floral display, certainly not above 65°F (18°C) by day and 55°F (13°C) at night.*

Water and food *The potting mix must be kept just moist but not wet. Feeding, though not essential, will encourage flowering in the garden the following year.*

Propagation *Offsets can be separated from the parent bulb when dormant, but commercially raised bulbs provide the biggest flower spikes and these should be bought annually in the fall.*

Hyacinths can be planted singly or in groups in bowls of potting mix or bulb fiber. Alternatively, they can be attractively grown and displayed in hyacinth glasses, which provide a lot of interest, especially to children.

Impatiens Wallerana hybrid

Impatiens

The Latin name *Impatiens* means impatient and refers to the seed pods which explode when touched or knocked, even when not thoroughly ripe. For the same reason, the commonly grown sorts, mostly forms of *I. Wallerana*, have acquired the vernacular name of Busy Lizzy. Why it is sometimes called Patient Lucy is a puzzle. It is a fleshy-stemmed shrub that bears lengthy succession of flat-faced flowers in shades of red, orange, pink, white and purple, sometimes with two of these colors.

Position *Bright light is necessary, ideally with a few hours of direct sunshine in all but the hottest summer months. A medium temperature of not less than 55°F (13°C) is tolerated but a warm temperature, 60°F (16°C) or above, is needed for winter blooming.*

Water and food *Water regularly but moderately, allowing the potting mix to dry at the surface between applications. Give liquid feed to established specimens at 10–14 day intervals from spring through fall.*

Propagation *Stem cuttings root readily at almost any time of the year. Seeds can be sown in a warm temperature, about 65–70°F (18–21°C).*

All too often the easy-going Busy Lizzy is left to itself and the result is a rather thin, lopsided specimen. To create a shapely plant, pinch out shoots of rooted cuttings when they reach 4–6 in (10–15 cm). As more shoots form, pinch out their tips in the same way.

Ixora coccinea

Ixora

The flame of the woods or jungle geranium, *I. coccinea*, is an ever-green shrub from India that can grow to 4 ft (1.2 m) in height and breadth in a tub but is easily kept to more manageable proportions in a smaller pot. Plants begin to flower when small.

Position *Bright light is necessary with several hours of direct sunshine each day, except in the height of summer. Warm temperatures, 60–70°F (16–21°C), are essential at all times.*

Water and food *Water regularly, but allow the surface of the potting mix to dry out between applications. Liquid feed at two- to three-weekly intervals, except in winter, is beneficial.*

Propagation *Take cuttings of firm young stems in spring or summer. Remove the soft tips and dip the stem bases into hormone rooting powder before potting. Keep the cuttings at a warm temperature of about 75°F (24°C).*

When an ixora has been potted-on to the largest convenient pot size, top dress the plant each year. First remove the top layer of potting mix with an old kitchen fork.

Replace the old mix with a layer of new, firming it round the plant to the same depth as before.

Jacobinia pauciflora

Jacobinia

One of the most attractive small species of this genus is *J. pauciflora*. It is a slender, small shrub, 1–2 ft (30–60 cm) tall, bearing a long succession of pendent, tubular, red and yellow flowers. *J. carnea* (Brazilian plume or pink acanthus) is robust, with thick erect stems 4 ft (1.2 m) tall or more, topped by dense spikes of rose-purple flowers.

Position *Bright light is vital for sturdy growth and good flowering. Normal room temperatures suit jacobinias during their active growth period. However, they must have a winter rest in a temperature of not less than 55°F (13°C).*
Water and food *Keep potting mix moist from spring to late fall, but during the rest period allow it almost to dry out between applications. Give liquid feed at two-weekly intervals during the growing season.*
Propagation *Cuttings of young growth root easily in spring or early summer in a warm temperature of about 65–70°F (18–21°C).*

Most jacobinias thrive in the home if a humid atmosphere is provided. To create high humidity, stand the plant on a tray of flooded gravel and spray the foliage each day.

Jasminum polyanthum

Jasminum

Common jasmine or jessamine, *J. officinale*, is one of the best known hardy twining climbers, long grown for its white, scented flowers. Superior in its production of pink-budded, white flowers and even more powerfully fragrant is the Chinese *J. polyanthum*. It tolerates room conditions surprisingly well and blooms from winter through spring. Non-twining and non-fragrant is the yellow-flowered primrose *J. Mesnyi* (*J. primulinum*), which blooms in spring and summer.

Position *Bright light is necessary if plants are to flower well.* J. Mesnyi *in particular requires several hours of direct sunshine each day and will benefit from spending the summer outdoors. A cool temperature in winter of not less than 45°F (7°C) must be provided to initiate a resting period.*
Water and food *Water regularly and freely in the growing season, but do not allow the potting mix to remain wet. Reduce the amount of water during the rest period. Liquid feed at two- to three-weekly intervals during the growing season.*
Propagation *Stem cuttings root readily in late summer or early fall without extra heat.*

A hoop or 'U'-shaped loop of bamboo or wire makes an efficient support for the stems of J. polyanthum. *At first, the stems will need tying in position but they will soon twine naturally.* J. Mesnyi *always needs tying in position.*

Justicia Brandegeana

Justicia

Although some 300 species are known in this genus, only one is widely grown. This is *J. Brandegeana*, also sometimes called *Beloperone* or *Drejerella* and popularly known as shrimp plant. It is a shrub which can be grown to 3 ft (1.2 m) in height or kept to under half this. It can even be grown as an annual from cuttings. The color of the flower spikes comes from the closely overlapping shrimp-pink bracts, from between which the slender white flowers protrude like tongues.

Position *Bright light is essential for sturdy plants, ideally with a few hours of direct sunshine, except during the hottest summer period. They are best kept in medium temperatures around 60°F (16°C).*

Water and food *Water moderately, at all times making sure that the potting mix is never saturated. Apply liquid feed at two-weekly intervals from spring through fall.*

Propagation *Take stem cuttings of shoot tips from plants cut back in late winter. They will grow rapidly and bloom in their second, if not first, year. Young plants need pinching out at intervals to promote a bushy habit.*

To keep compact and under 1½ ft (45 cm) in height, annual pruning is recommended. Do this in late winter to spring. First, cut all the main stems back by two thirds, then all the small side stems (laterals) to 1 in (2.5 cm), severing at a node or leaf. Apply a top dressing of potting mix soon afterwards to encourage new growth.

Kalanchoe Blossfeldiana

Kalanchoe

This genus comprises mostly shrubby plants, with thick fleshy leaves and terminal clusters of tubular, four-petalled flowers. Best known are the forms and hybrids of *K. Blossfeldiana*. A bushy plant to about 1 ft (30 cm), it produces a profusion of flowers in shades of red and yellow in fall and winter.

Position *Bright light is essential, with at least a half day of direct sunshine daily, particularly in winter and spring. A medium temperature of not less than 50–55°F (10–13°C) is needed for winter flowering.*

Water and food *Water regularly, but allow the potting mix almost to dry out between applications. If the temperature drops as low as 50°F (10°C), keep almost dry. Liquid feed once a month.*

Propagation *Cuttings root readily at all times, but are best taken in spring. A warm temperature of at least 65°F (18°C) hastens rooting.*

Cuttings of K. Bloss-feldiana should be of non-flowering basal or side shoots, each with two pairs of leaves.

Dip each cutting in rooting powder but leave it for 24 hours to dry before planting in potting mix.

Kohleria eriantha

Kohleria

Erect in growth and sometimes almost shrubby, kohlerias have attractive, velvety, hairy stems and leaves, and a long succession of slightly inflated tubular flowers in shades of red, pink, yellow or white. *K. eriantha*, also called *Isoloma hirsuta*, is the best known, with orange-red, 2 in (5 cm) long flowers in summer.

Position *Bright light keeps the plants sturdy and flowering well. Direct sunshine is beneficial but should be screened in summer. These plants tolerate high temperatures in summer but store rhizomes when dormant in a cool temperature of 45–50°F (7–10°C).*

Water and food *Water very sparingly when the rhizomes are first potted in spring. When in full growth, water regularly but allow the top of the potting mix to dry out between applications. Reduce the amount of water after flowering. Apply liquid feed at two-weekly intervals when in full growth and until flowering ceases.*

Propagation *The natural increase of the scaly rhizomes each year makes propagation automatic.*

The scaly rhizomes, or tubers as they are sometimes called, should be handled with care. In spring plant three or four in a 5 in (13 cm) pot and cover them with about 1½ in (4 cm) of potting mix. To establish them quickly and successfully, a minimum temperature of 65–70°F (18–21°C) is recommended.

Lachenalia aloides

Lachenalia

Popularly known as Cape cowslips, the lachenalias are perhaps the most decorative of all the small, tender, bulbous plants. They are easily grown in a sunny window and, depending on temperature, flower from late winter through spring.

Position *Bright light is absolutely essential, with as much direct sunshine as possible. These plants cannot tolerate cool temperatures.*

Water and food *When potted in fall the bulbs need one good watering, then none until the foliage shows. Thereafter, water regularly but allow the potting mix to dry partially between applications. When leaves die down, stop watering. Apply liquid feed at two-weekly intervals once the leaves are well grown and until they start to fade.*

Propagation *Separate offsets at re-potting time and grow on separately.*

Since they grow naturally in well-drained soils, lachenalias must be planted in a free-draining potting mix. Place a layer of crocks in the bottom of the pot to help drainage.

Half fill a container 5 in (15 cm) wide and deep with a porous, ideally sandy mix. Set five or six bulbs into this layer.

Cover the bulbs with a layer of potting mix so that their tops are at least 1½ in (4 cm) below the surface. Water the bulbs and keep them at 55–60°F (13–16°C).

Lantana Camara

Lantana

Yellow sage, *L. Camara*, is popular in the gardens of warm countries and makes a most attractive plant in a pot, especially the popular dwarf forms that rarely exceed 1 ft (30 cm) or so. Yellow, orange, pink, red and white are the basic colors, and usually the color changes from one to another as the bud opens into the flower.

Position *Bright light is necessary, with at least a few hours of direct sunshine daily. These plants tolerate most temperatures but in winter they must rest in a medium temperature, no less than 50°F (10°C), for six to eight weeks.*

Water and food *Water regularly to keep the potting mix moist but not wet. In winter, allow the potting mix almost to dry out between applications. Apply liquid feed every two weeks during the growing period.*

Propagation *If placed in a temperature of about 65–70°F (18–21°C), cuttings taken in late summer root readily. Alternatively sow seed in spring at the same temperature.*

The larger forms of lantana can become sizeable shrubs and straggly with age. A regular late winter pruning will prevent this. Cut back all the strong stems of the previous year by two thirds and the remaining, thinner stems to 2 in (5 cm).

Liriope Muscari

Liriope

The genus Liriope is native to eastern Asia and contains only six species. Several have become popular as outdoor ground cover in warmer climates and indoors as pot plants. They have acquired the vernacular name of lilytuft, as the smaller spreading sorts form a sward like rough grass. All have slender, grassy but leathery and glossy leaves and spikes of tiny bell-shaped flowers. The only species showy enough in bloom to be included here is *L. Muscari*. It is clump-forming and reaches about 1 ft (30 cm) with lilac to violet flowers in fall.

Position *Bright light is required but direct sunshine is not essential. Liriopes tolerate high temperatures in summer but must be given a cool winter rest at a temperature of 40–50°F (5–10°C).*

Water and food *Water regularly to keep the potting mix moist but never wet; give less in winter. Liquid feed once a month during the growing period.*

Propagation *Divide clumps during late winter or spring.*

L. Muscari *resents disturbance and only congested specimens should be divided. Turn the plant out of its pot and split the root ball with a knife.*

Each division must have at least three to four shoots. Pot the divisions singly, firming the potting mix round the plant.

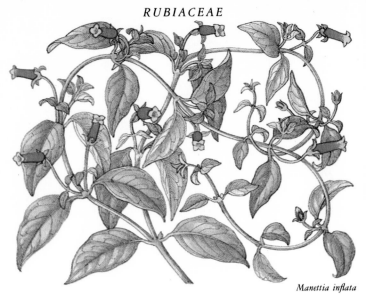

Manettia inflata

Manettia

The only species grown indoors is *M. inflata* (*M. bicolor*), an evergreen twining climber to about 4 ft (1.2 m), with rich, green, lustrous oval leaves and tubular flowers. The flowers are about ¾ in (1.8 cm) long, scarlet with a bright yellow tip.

Position *Bright light is needed but not direct sunlight. Allow plants to rest in winter in a medium temperature of not less than 55–60°F (13–16°C).*

Water and food *The potting mix must be maintained in a moist state throughout the year but not allowed to remain over-wet. Apply liquid feed at two-weekly intervals from late spring through fall.*

Propagation *Take cuttings of non-flowering shoot tips at any time from spring to late summer. They will root readily in a warm temperature of 65–70°F (18–21°C).*

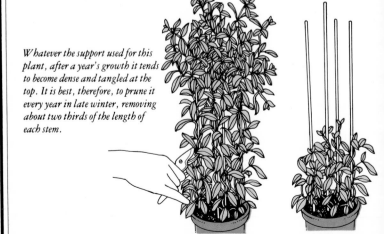

Whatever the support used for this plant, after a year's growth it tends to become dense and tangled at the top. It is best, therefore, to prune it every year in late winter, removing about two thirds of the length of each stem.

Narcissus hybrid

Narcissus

Daffodils and narcissi are both members of this genus. The key character for deciding which is which is the length of the trumpet or cup. This must be of equal or greater length than the petals to qualify it as a trumpet daffodil. Most of the commonly grown narcissi and daffodils are of complicated hybrid origin and are known by cultivar names. The majority are hardy garden plants but they can also be used as short-term house plants. The bulbs must be potted and cared for as described under *Hyacinthus*.

Position *Bright light is needed to keep the plants sturdy and a few hours of direct sunshine daily is beneficial. Cool conditions are essential if the flowers are to last for more than a few days. A night temperature around 50°F (10°C) should be aimed at, with a day maximum of 65°F (18°C).*

Water and food *Keep the soil just moist but not wet. Feeding is not essential but will encourage flowering in the garden in the following year.*

Propagation *Separate offsets during the dormant period. Newly purchased bulbs must be planted each year for a good display in the home.*

Bulbs can be planted in potting mix or, if they are to be discarded after flowering, sterile media such as coconut (bulb) fiber and shingle (pebbles, gravel) can be used. Shingle is particularly attractive.

Almost fill bowls 3 in (7.5 cm) deep with shingle. Set the bulbs into the shingle and maintain the water level just below the bulb bases.

Pachystachys lutea

Pachystachys

Of the six species of evergreen shrubs and perennials in this genus only one, *P. lutea*, is now widely grown as a pot plant. It has become popular only since 1964, when it was introduced from Peru by T. H. Everett, then the Senior Horticulture Specialist at the New York Botanical Garden. It is an erect shrub that reaches 4 ft (1.2 m) or more if grown in a large container, but makes a neat plant about 1½ ft (45 cm) tall if grown annually from cuttings. The showy yellow of the summer-borne flower spikes is provided by bracts.

Position *Bright light is needed for sturdy growth and flowering is best in a position with a few hours of direct sunshine daily. A medium temperature, minimum 55–60°F (13–16°C), is required.*

Water and food *Water regularly but do not allow the potting mix to remain permanently wet. Apply liquid feed at two-weekly intervals during the summer growing period.*

Propagation *Cuttings of young growth from plants cut back in early spring root readily in a warm temperature of 66–70°F (18–21°C).*

The showy yellow part of the flower spike of P. lutea *is provided by bracts. These are not part of the flower but are derived from leaves. The true flowers are small and white and they push their way out from between the bracts. Although each flower only lasts a few days, the bracts remain attractive for several months.*

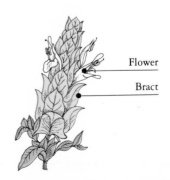

Flower

Bract

Passiflora caerulea

Passiflora

The blossoms of *P. caerulea*, the blue passionflower, are unique in the plant world. Missionaries to the New World saw them as symbols of Christ's crucifixion, for from the center of each flower rises a stalk, bearing a ring of large stamens (the five wounds) and an ovary surmounted by several stigmas (the three nails). In the center is a ring of filaments (the crown of thorns).

Position *Bright light is essential, with at least a half day in direct sunshine except during the hottest summer period. This plant must be given a cool winter rest between 45–50°F (7–10°C).*

Water and food *The potting mix must be kept moist at all times but never wet. Water less in winter. Liquid feed at two-weekly intervals from late spring to fall.*

Propagation *Stem cuttings roots easily from late winter through summer, in a warm temperature of 65–70°F (18–21°C). Alternatively, sow at the same temperature in spring.*

A 'U'-shaped loop of bamboo or wire makes the best support for a passiflora. Since the plant is strong growing and naturally grows straight up, it needs to be tied in to follow the shape of the frame. The strong tendrils, which entwine around leaves and stems as well as the support, are best removed.

Pelargonium × *domesticum* variety

Pelargonium × domesticum

T his name covers the so-called regal, fancy or show geraniums or pelargoniums. They are shrubby plants, usually of stiff, compact habit to about 2 ft (60 cm) tall, with sharply-toothed, rounded leaves that are usually somewhat cupped. The flowers are larger than those of the more familiar pot or zonal geranium.

Position *As much direct sunlight as possible is needed, with a little shade during the hottest part of the summer. Medium or warm temperatures suit these plants in summer but they need a winter rest at a medium temperature of around 50°F (10°C).*

Water and food *During the growing season water regularly, but allow the surface of the potting mix to dry out between applications. Little water is needed in winter. Give liquid feed to established plants at two-weekly intervals during the growing season.*

Propagation *Take cuttings in summer, when they will root fairly readily.*

After one or two growing seasons, pelargoniums may have lost their lower leaves and become leggy. For this reason they are best cut back regularly in late winter by removing at least two thirds of the top growth. This will not only maintain a shorter, bushier plant but will encourage the growth of vigorous shoots ideal for cuttings.

GERANIACEAE

Pelargonium × hortorum variety

Pelargonium × hortorum

All the many common, pot or zonal geraniums come under this hybrid name. Some cultivars have a bronze to brownish horseshoe-shaped leaf marking but most modern kinds have plain green foliage.

Position *Keep these plants in bright light, with as much direct sunlight as possible. They will tolerate most summer temperatures but need a cool winter rest at a temperature of about 45°F (7°C).*

Water and food *Except in mid-winter when amounts should be greatly reduced, water regularly but allow the potting mix to become partially dry between applications.*

Propagation *Cuttings root readily from spring through late summer, if screened from direct sunshine.*

Zonal geraniums make good standards. Keep young plants growing vigorously. Remove any shoots that arise in the leaf axils. When the main stem has reached the desired height, allow three more leaves to develop then remove the growing point. Shoots will develop from these upper leaf axils and must in turn be pinched out when they have four to six leaves.

Pentas lanceolata

Pentas

The only member of this genus to be used as a house plant is *P. lanceolata*, the star-cluster, sometimes referred to as *P. carnea*. It is a shrub that grows up to 5 ft (1.5 m) tall but is easily kept much smaller and can be grown annually from cuttings.

Position *Keep these plants in bright light where they receive several hours of direct sunshine daily. A warm minimum temperature of about 60°F (16°C) at night must be maintained for flowering.*

Water and food *Water regularly during the growing season, but allow the potting mix to dry at the surface between applications. Reduce the amount of water during the rest period. Liquid feed at two-week intervals during the summer and fall is recommended.*

Propagation *Cuttings of non-flowering shoots, preferably from cut back plants, root readily at any time.*

P. lanceolata *grows tall and must be pruned annually to keep it under 2 ft (60 cm). In early spring, cut away three quarters of all the previous season's growth. This will make for a compact plant and will encourage new growth.*

Plumbago auriculata

Plumbago

With its long succession of sky-blue, primrose-shaped flowers, *P. auriculata*, the cape leadwort, is one of the best loved of all greenhouse climbers. Better known under its former name *P. capensis*, it is a tolerant plant and responds well to home conditions.

Position *Bright light with several hours of direct sunshine daily is essential for good flowering. This plant will thrive in most temperatures but must be given a cool temperature in winter of 45–50°F (7–10°C) to allow a rest period.*
Water and food *Water regularly to keep the potting mix moist but never wet. Less water is required during winter. Give liquid feed at two- to three-weekly intervals during the growing period.*
Propagation *Semi-hardwood cuttings, ideally with a heel of parent stem attached, root fairly readily if taken in spring or summer and kept in a warm temperature of about 65–70°F (18–21°C).*

This plumbago does not twine or bear tendrils so needs to be tied to its support. Push three or four 3–4 ft (90–120 cm) canes into the potting mix near the edge of the pot. Wind the stems carefully round in spiral fashion, tying them to each cane.

Primula obconica

Primula

This large and decorative genus provides garden and greenhouse plants as well as several that make splendid pot plants for the home. The most popular house plant is *P. malacoides*, the fairy primrose, with its elegant tiers of mauve, pink, red or white flowers that appear in winter and spring. Well grown plants can be 1–1½ ft (30–45 cm) tall. Also attractive is *P. obconica*, sometimes known as German or poison primrose as it can cause an irritant skin rash. It is more massive than *P. malacoides*, with flowers in shades of pink, red, blue or white and is the only house plant species that can be kept for a second year.

Position *Direct sunshine is essential, with at least some in the mid-fall through mid-spring period. These plants must be kept at a medium temperature of 50–55°F (10–13°C). Higher temperatures will shorten the flowering period.*
Water and food *Water regularly but do not allow the potting mix to remain constantly wet. Feed at two-weekly intervals in late winter, weekly in spring.*
Propagation *Try sowing seed in spring or summer, although it is not easy to raise good plants in the home.* P. obconica *can be divided after flowering.*

Nothing detracts more from a flowering pot plant than brown, withered or dying flowers. Inspect primulas every two or three days, removing the flowers as soon as they start to wilt and hang down. If seed is to be saved, leave some of the faded flowers intact.

Punica Granatum nana

Punica

The pomegranate, *P. Granatum*, is well known as a fruiting shrub in frost-free climates but is too large for the home. It has, however, produced a dwarf sport (mutant) *P.g. nana*, which is not only a perfect miniature but is evergreen and makes a decorative house plant. Easily kept to about 1½ ft (45 cm) or less, it has glossy narrow leaves and bears a long succession of orange-red flowers in late spring through summer. The latter are bell-shaped, about 1 in (2.5 cm) long, and appear at the tips of the branches. Flowers are followed by yellow to orange fruits about 2 in (5 cm) in diameter.

Position *During the growing season at least, bright light with several hours of direct sunlight daily is vital. Poor light is tolerated in winter. Average home temperatures suit the plant in spring and summer but it must be allowed to rest in winter at a cool temperature of less than 50°F (10°C).*

Water and food *Give enough water to keep the potting mix moist but not wet during the growing season. Less is required in winter. Give liquid feed every two weeks during the summer.*

Propagation *Cuttings with a heel of parent stem taken in mid- to late summer root satisfactorily. Older stems can be layered in spring.*

Take heel cuttings just as the shoot bases start to become woody. Grasp the potential cutting at the base with thumb and forefinger and carefully pull back and down. Trim the 'tail' of bark before potting the cutting in potting mix.

Rebutia minuscula

Rebutia

This genus of desert cacti is renowned for its free flowering, even from an early age. All are small plants with cylindrical to globular stems, which may be solitary or form clumps. Unlike some larger desert cacti, the flowers are borne near ground level and may form a complete ring around the base of the plant. Red, orange and yellow are the main flower colors. Particularly satisfactory is the diminutive *R. minuscula*, commonly known as red-crown, which forms clusters of stems which reach 2 in (6 cm) in height and bears red flowers.

Position *Bright light is essential, with as much direct sunshine as possible, except during the hottest summer period when light shade is appreciated. Any summer temperatures are suitable but these plants must have a winter rest at a cool temperature of 36–40°F (2–4°C) if abundant flowers are to be produced.*
Water and food *From spring through fall, water regularly but allow the potting mix almost to dry between the applications. Keep almost dry in winter. During active growth in summer, give liquid feed at two-weekly intervals.*
Propagation *Separate offsets either in spring or after flowering in summer. Alternatively, seeds germinate freely if sown in a warm temperature, about 70°F (21°C). They will reach flowering size in 12–18 months.*

About 25 species are known in this cactus genus, all native to southern Bolivia and northern Argentina. They vary greatly in overall appearance and size. Very few are above 3 in (7.5 cm) in height and most are even smaller.

R. haggei

R. senilis

R. violaciflora

Rhododendron simsii

Rhododendron

The only rhododendron commonly available as a house plant is *R. simsii* and its hybrid cultivars, known often as Indian azalea. It is a bushy shrub growing to 2 ft (60 cm) or more, with small elliptic leaves and terminal trusses of wide funnel-shaped flowers about 2 in (5 cm) across. These may be red, pink, purple or white, and sometimes are bicolored.

Position *Bright light is necessary, but avoid direct sunshine. Cool conditions are essential for a prolonged display of flowers. A minimum of 45°F (7°C) and a maximum of about 65°F (18°C) is ideal.*

Water and food *Water regularly with soft, lime-free water to keep the potting mix moist but not wet. Humidity is essential. Apply liquid feed at two- to three-weekly intervals during the growing season. From spring through fall, stand the plant outside in a shady place.*

Propagation *Root stem tip cuttings in late spring in a propagating case in a warm temperature of 65°F (18°C) or layer in fall or spring.*

Rhododendrons come from areas of high rainfall and humidity. To provide humidity to plants flowering indoors, stand the pot on a tray of flooded gravel or small pebbles, or plunge the pot into a larger container of moist peat (right). The latter method has the added advantage of keeping the roots cool, an important factor in keeping rhododendrons healthy in the home.

Rochea coccinea

Rochea

The few species in this genus are small shrubs from South Africa. Technically they are succulents, but the small, firm, somewhat lustrous leaves are only slightly fleshy. *R. coccinea* is the species usually available and can make a shrub to 2 ft (60 cm) in height. It is best grown annually from cuttings, when it will be half this in size and nicely bushy if pinched regularly when young.

Position *Bright light is essential, with as much direct sunshine as possible. These plants tolerate any summer temperature but must be encouraged to rest in winter at a medium temperature of 50°F (10°C).*

Water and food *During the growing season, water regularly but allow the potting mix to dry out partially between applications. Little water is needed in winter. Liquid feed should be given at two-weekly intervals, once the young flower buds show. Stop feeding at the end of the flowering period.*

Propagation *Stem cuttings root easily in spring or summer. They do not require high humidity.*

Like many other perennial pot plants, rocheas soon become straggly if they are not pruned. If a plant is to be kept for more than one year or if cuttings are required, cut it back hard in late winter (right). The resulting compact shrub (far right) will soon produce new growth.

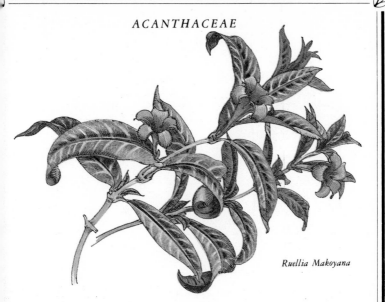

Ruellia Makoyana

Ruellia

About 250 species of perennials and shrubs are listed for this genus but only two or three are widely cultivated and only one is grown as a house plant. All have long tubular flowers with five flared petal lobes, which emerge directly from the upper leaf axils. Several species have decorative leaves. In *R. Makoyana*, the monkey or trailing velvet plant, they are rich, satiny, olive-green above with a silvery vein pattern. The leaf undersurfaces are rich purple and some of this color shows through. The rosy carmine flowers are about 2 in (5 cm) long and open from the fall through spring.

Position *Bright light is necessary with shading in summer from strong sunlight. A warm temperature in winter of 60°F (16°C) is needed for flowering, but 55°F (13°C) is tolerated.*

Water and food *Water regularly but moderately, allowing the surface of the potting mix to dry out between applications. An almost dry rest period of about six weeks, starting when flowering ceases, is recommended. Give liquid feed at two-weekly intervals during the growing season.*

Propagation *Cuttings, ideally of non-flowering stem tips, root readily in a warm temperature of about 70°F (21°C). Summer is the best time.*

R. Makoyana looks at its best in a hanging basket. Thickly line the basket with sphagnum moss and fill it with an all-peat potting mix. Plant three ruellias into a 10 in (25 cm) basket.

Saintpaulia ionantha

Saintpaulia

Such is the popularity of saintpaulias, or African violets, that growers have formed societies. Only very few of the 21 species are widely grown, but these have numerous mutant forms and cultivated varieties that differ widely in leaf shape and flower color and size. Flowers may be single or double, in shades of blue, purple, red, pink or white. There are now miniature saintpaulias, largely of hybrid origin bred from some of the naturally tiny species. All species come from the drier parts of East Africa, growing in the shade of rocks or other plants.

Position *Keep these plants in moderately bright light, out of hot direct sunshine which can scorch the leaves. They thrive only in warm temperatures. A minimum of 60°F (16°C) is tolerated but 65–70°F (18–21°C) is ideal.*

Water and food *Water in moderation, letting the potting mix almost dry out between applications. Care must be taken not to wet the leaves. Give liquid feed at every watering, ideally one of the proprietary brands made for saintpaulias.*

Propagation *Division or leaf cuttings are the usual and easiest methods, ideally in late spring or early summer.*

Breeders of saintpaulias have created a vast range of attractive hybrids to give the grower endless choice of flower color and form. This small selection of named hybrids may not be available everywhere but similar types will certainly be found.

S. 'Rhapsodie Venus'   S. 'Ballet Eva'   S. 'Rhapsodie Gigi'   S. 'Coral Caper'   S. 'Blue Nimbus'

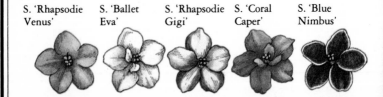

Schlumbergera truncata

Schlumbergera

The best known species in this genus of tropical forest cacti is still often referred to as *Zygocactus truncatus*, though it is now 30 years since the two genera were united. Schlumbergeras are air plants (epiphytes), found perching on branches and mossy rocks in the forests of Brazil. What appear to be jointed leaves are really flattened stems, but they carry out the functions of leaves. In *S. truncata* (crab cactus) each joint has large, pointed teeth. In *S. Bridgesii* (Christmas cactus) the joints have shallow, rounded teeth. All flower in winter.

Position *Except in winter, direct sunlight must be screened but bright light is needed for sturdy growth and good flowering. A warm temperature of at least 60°F (16°C) is required for winter blooming.*

Water and food *Water regularly, letting the potting mix almost dry out between applications. After flowering, keep almost dry for about six weeks to allow a rest period.*

Propagation *Cuttings, each consisting of two joints, root readily in spring or summer if kept at a warm temperature of 65–70°F (18–21°C).*

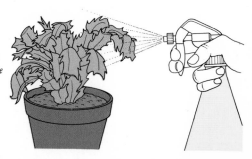

Schlumbergeras thrive in a humid atmosphere. Increase humidity, especially in spring and summer, by spraying them each day with rain water. Harder water contains too much calcium for these plants.

Sinningia speciosa hybrid

Sinningia

The most popular species in this genus, *S. speciosa*, has given rise to many forms all commonly called gloxinias, although they are nothing to do with the genus of the same name. They grow from almost woody, rounded tubers, producing a tuft or rosette of oval, hairy leaves. The leaves are handsome and large, up to 8 in (20 cm) or so in length.

Position *Medium to bright light is needed but not direct sunshine, which can mark the leaves. A warm temperature of 60–65°F (16–18°C) must be provided to encourage growth. Store dormant tubers dry at no lower than 55°F (13°C).*

Water and food *Water sparingly when the tubers are started into growth in spring. Later, keep the potting mix moist but allow the surface to dry out between applications. Reduce the amount as winter approaches. Keep dry in winter.*

Propagation *Cut tubers into pieces when growth starts, or use the shoots as cuttings. Alternatively, take leaf cuttings in summer or sow seeds in spring.*

If you want more young plants than you can make by dividing the tubers, try taking leaf cuttings. Select fully mature leaves but not those that are old.

Cut each leaf into three or four transverse sections. Use a sharp knife or razor blade for this to prevent bruising the leaf tissue.

Place the leaf sections in containers of equal parts peat and sand, inserting them obliquely with the lower third buried; then very gently firm the mix.

Smithiantha × hybrida

Smithiantha

Temple-bells is the charmingly apt name for this Mexican genus. The plants are sturdily erect, with terminal spikes of bell-shaped flowers rising to 2 ft (60 cm) or more in height. If the scaly rhizomes are potted at four-weekly intervals from late winter through spring, flowers will bloom throughout summer and fall. *S. zebrina* has handsome dark green leaves with a purplish vein pattern. It has passed on these characteristics to some of its popular hybrid cultivars, which carry flowers in shades of red, pink, orange, yellow and white.

Position *Medium to bright light is needed, but direct sunshine, especially in summer, can scorch the leaves. A warm temperature of not less than 60–65°F (16–18°C) is vital. Store the dormant rhizomes in a medium temperature of about 55°F (13°C).*
Water and food *Water sparingly when the tubers are started into growth. Later, keep the potting mix moist but allow the surface to dry out between applications. After flowering, water less until plants die down. Keep dormant rhizomes dry. Give liquid feed every two weeks in the growing season.*
Propagation *Rhizomes increase naturally each year.*

The scaly rhizomes of smithiantha are much like those of achimenes but larger. Plant three rhizomes in a 5 in (13 cm) container to produce an attractively full pot by summer.

Sparmannia africana

Sparmannia

Also known as African hemp and indoor linden (lime), sparmannia has handsome, maple-like hairy leaves to 6 in (15 cm) long on equally long stalks. The pure white flowers are about 1½ in (4 cm) wide, each with a collection of yellow and purple stamens in the center.

Position *Bright light is necessary with several hours of direct sunshine daily, except in the summer when it should be lightly screened. A medium temperature of 50–60°F (10–16°C) suits this plant throughout the year.*

Water and food *Water regularly during the growing season but do not let the potting mix remain wet. In winter, keep the plant on the dry side. Feed well-established plants at two-weekly intervals during the summer.*

Propagation *Cuttings taken in spring, preferably from plants cut back in winter, root readily in a warm temperature of about 65°F (18°C).*

Sparmannias can easily become leggy and untidy, so it is best to start controlling them when young. Pinch out rooted cuttings when they reach 4–6 in (10–15 cm).

When the three to four shoots that arise from the first pinching each has about four leaves, remove their tips.

If large bushy plants are required, all the shoots that grow after the second pinching should be pinched out when they have four to six leaves.

Spathiphyllum Clevelandii

Spathiphyllum

The 35 species of evergreen tropical perennials in this genus are similar to species of *Zantedeschia* but are more graceful. Slender stems carry open, pure white spathes, each surrounding a cylindrical club of tiny yellow flowers. *S. Clevelandii* has glossy oblong leaves to 10 in (25 cm) long and 1–1½ ft (30–45 cm) tall flower stems bearing 5–6 in (13–15 cm) long spathes. *S.* × 'Mauna Loa' is more robust, with larger leaves and spathes to 8 in (20 cm) long on 2 ft (60 cm) tall stems, borne in spring and summer.

Position *Medium to bright light is needed but screen direct sunlight, except in winter. A medium temperature of at least 55°F (13°C) is necessary.*
Water and food *Water regularly, just enough to keep the potting mix moist but not wet. Less water is needed in winter. Apply liquid feed at two-weekly intervals during the growing season and keep humidity high.*
Propagation *Divide well-clumped specimens in spring.*

The spathiphyllums described here are either inhabitants of humid tropical climates or are hybrids that need the same conditions. Initially, stand a plant on a tray of flooded gravel or plunge its pot into a large container of moist peat. In addition, moisten the foliage daily with a mist spray.

ASCLEPIADACEAE

Stephanotis floribunda

Stephanotis

Only one species in this genus of 15 tropical climbers is grown as a house plant. This is *S. floribunda*, the Madagascar jasmine or wax flower. Its powerfully fragrant, waxy-textured white flowers, like those of a huge jasmine, are used in floral arrangements. The stems can twine to several meters in length, but in a small pot can be kept shorter.

Position *Bright light is necessary and direct winter sunshine is recommended. At other times it must be screened. A medium temperature of at least 55°F (13°C) is suitable but higher temperatures are preferable during the growing season.*

Water and food *Keep the potting mix moist but not wet at all times. Give liquid feed at two-week intervals during the growing season.*

Propagation *Cuttings root moderately well if a warm temperature of not less than 65–70°F (18–21°C) is maintained. Use non-flowering lateral shoots in the spring.*

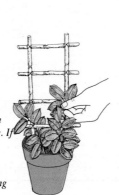

The stems of stephanotis will twine around their supports, but will need tying in position to train them down the other side. If you want a large, full plant, pinch out the growing tips of a young plant to induce branching low down.

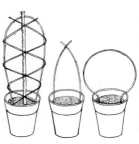

A wide variety of supports are suitable; some of the most useful are shown here. Another good example is the simple inverted 'U'.

Streptocarpus × *hybridus*

Streptocarpus

There are three different growth forms in this large African genus of some 130 species: shrub-like, with almost fleshy stems; rosette (or tufted), and solitary-leaved. The last group is unique in the plant world, plants bearing one leaf only. Most popular are the rosetted sorts, represented by *S.* × *hybridus* (Cape primrose), which bears foxglove-like flowers in shades of blue, purple, red, pink and white.

Position *Bright light is best but direct sunlight should be screened, except during winter. A medium temperature, of at least 50°F (10°C), is tolerated but 60°F (16°C) or above is best.*

Water and food *Water regularly but allow the surface of the potting mix to dry out between applications. If temperatures become cool, below 50°F (10°C), keep almost dry.*

Propagation *Leaf cuttings, seeds or division are the main methods for the rosetted sorts. All require a warm temperature of about 65°F (18°C).*

All the popular cultivars of streptocarpus regenerate freely from leaves. The standard method is to cut mature leaves transversely into 1½–2 in (4–5 cm) long sections, then to insert them in the potting mix obliquely to a depth of one third. A half peat and half sand mix is best.

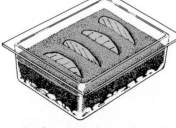

An alternative method is to slice out the mid-rib of each leaf (left) and to insert the longitudinal halves in an almost erect position (above), burying the lower part to one third its depth.

Tibouchina Urvilleana

Tibouchina

Only one species in this genus, *T. Urvilleana*, often mis-identified as *T. semidecandra*, is widely grown. From summer through early winter it carries a succession of satiny-textured, rich blue-purple, saucer-shaped flowers, each about 3 in (7.5 cm) wide. Although this shrub can attain 10 ft (3 m) or more in a large container, it is easily kept to 2–3 ft (60–90 cm) if pruned each spring.

Position *Bright light is needed, with direct sunshine from mid-fall to mid-spring. Normal room temperatures suit tibouchinas during the growing period. Allow plants to rest in winter at a medium temperature of about 50°F (10°C), or just below.*

Water and food *Except during the rest period, keep the potting mix moist but not wet. In winter, keep on the dry side. Apply liquid feed at two- to three-weekly intervals from early summer through fall.*

Propagation *Stem cuttings root readily from late spring through late summer in a warm temperature of at least 70°F (21°C).*

Take stem or tip cuttings of firm lateral stems from the parent plant in spring. Each cutting should have about three pairs of leaves.

Trim beneath a node and remove the lowest pair of leaves. Then dip the stem in rooting powder that contains fungicide.

Plant the cutting in a small pot of potting mix, then enclose pot and cutting in a plastic bag to maintain high humidity.

Tulipa hybrid

Tulipa

Tulips have been important garden plants for centuries. In addition to the conservative estimate of 50 wild species, there are many hundreds of cultivated varieties in a wide range of heights, flower forms and colors. Some of these make splendid short-term pot plants. Pot the bulbs in mid- to late October so that the nose of each bulb is set just above the potting mix. When potted keep them as cool as possible, at least down to 50°F (10°C) at night until the shoots appear. This aids the build up of an extensive root system and ensures good flowering.

Position *Bright light is essential once the shoots appear and several hours of direct sunshine each day are beneficial. Cool conditions are vital, however, ideally not above 65–70°F (18–21°C) by day and down to at least 55°F (13°C) at night.*

Water and food *Keep the potting mix just moist but not wet at all times; dryness can cause the buds to shrivel. Feeding is not essential, but it is worthwhile if bulbs are to be planted in a garden after flowering indoors.*

Propagation *Separate offsets when dormant, but buy commercially raised bulbs annually for a good floral display.*

Although tulip bulbs will flower if planted in bulb (coconut) fiber, a properly formulated potting mix gives the best results. Plant bulbs in a bowl 3–4 in (7.5–10 cm) deep so that the tips are just showing. Keep them cool until well rooted.

Vallota speciosa

Vallota

This genus contains only one species, *V. speciosa* (sometimes called *V. purpurea*), the Scarborough lily, a native of South Africa, where it is called Berg or George lily. Resembling a smaller, more refined *Hippeastrum*, it is an evergreen bulbous plant that eventually forms small clumps. The 2¾–4 in (7–10 cm) long flowers open during summer and early fall. Flowers are usually scarlet, but *V.s.* 'Delicata' is a pale salmon-pink and *V.s.* 'Alba' is entirely white. *V.s.* 'Magnifica' is scarlet, with a white eye.

Position *Bright light is essential, with at least some direct sunlight during the mid-fall through spring period. They thrive in most indoor temperatures but they must have a winter rest in a medium temperature of about 50°F (10°C).*
Water and food *Water regularly in the growing season but make sure the potting mix never remains constantly wet. Water sparingly in winter, keeping the potting mix almost dry. Apply liquid feed at two- to three-week intervals from mid-spring through mid-fall.*
Propagation *Separate offsets from well-clumped plants in spring.*

Offsets are freely produced by vallotas and can be separated from the parent plant. However, if only one or two larger, flowering-sized plants are required it is best to divide large, congested plants (right) after flowering or in spring. Remove the rootball from the pot and pull clumps apart (far right). Pot each clump separately.

Veltheimia viridifolia

Veltheimia

Best known in this genus, and the one usually grown as a house plant, is *V. viridifolia*. It is sometimes erroneously called *V. capensis*. It has rich, glossy green leaves to 15 in (38 cm) and stems to 1½ ft (45 cm) tall, bearing red flowers in spring. *V.v.* 'Rosealba' has beautiful, pink-flushed white flowers. *V. capensis* has shorter, gray-green leaves and smaller, pale pink flowers in winter.

Position *Bright light is necessary and these plants must have a few hours daily of direct sunshine. Veltheimias do not appreciate heat. A warm temperature of less than 60°F (16°C) must be maintained, especially in winter which is unusually the growing period.*

Water and food *After potting in early fall, water sparingly. Once the leaves start to grow, water regularly but allow the top of the potting mix to dry between applications. In late spring, V. capensis must be dried off and V. viridifolia kept only just moist during the summer (it is normally evergreen). Give liquid feed at two-weekly intervals once the leaves are fully grown.*

Propagation *Remove offsets when bulbs are re-potted after two or three years growth.*

Removing offsets is the easiest way to increase veltheimias, though production is never abundant. Remove each offset only when it separates readily from the parent bulb. Pot three or four offsets together. They will flower after about three years growth.

Zantedeschia albomaculata

Zantedeschia

The best known species of zantedeschia is calla lily, *Z. aethiopica*, with stems of 3 ft (90 cm) or more and pure white spathes 6–10 in (15–25 cm) long. *Z.a.* 'Childsiana' is more compact and makes a much better house plant. *Z.a.* 'Green Goddess' has spathes flushed green. *Z. albomaculata*, the spotted calla, has translucently white spotted leaves and pale yellow spathes with red-purple throats. All zantedeschias grow actively through winter and bear flowers in late winter or spring.

Position *Bright light is necessary, with a few hours of direct sunlight daily.*
Water and food *When newly potted in fall, water the rhizomes sparingly but, as the leaves grow, keep the potting mix moist although never wet. Four to six weeks after flowering has finished, all but* Z. aethiopica *should be dried off. This species is best kept just moist during its rest period. When in full growth, apply liquid feed at two-weekly intervals.*
Propagation *Separate offsets or divide clumps when re-potting in the fall.*

Z. aethiopica *produces plenty of offsets and, if grown on in large pots, will form big clumps. Divide the rhizomes just as the young growth starts, ensuring that each division has a growing point (right). Plant the divided rhizomes, and they should flower the same season.*

Glossary

Words in *italic* type denote other Glossary entries.

Active growth period That time in the year when a plant grows and develops new leaves and flowers. Compare *Dormant* and *Resting*.

Air plant See *Epiphyte*.

Annual A plant that grows from seed, flowers, produces seed and dies within the space of a single growing season. Compare *Biennial* and *Perennial*.

Axil The angle between a leaf or leafstalk and the stem from which it grows.

Biennial A plant that grows from seed, flowers, produces seed and dies within the space of two growing seasons. Compare *Annual* and *Perennial*.

Bract A modified leaf or part of a flower, often highly colored and of long duration.

Bulb A storage organ, usually growing beneath ground, that in its *dormant* state contains the plant's embryo leaves and flowers.

Corm An underground storage organ, formed from the base of a plant's stem.

Cutting A leaf or portion of a leaf, or stem severed from a plant and used to produce a new plant.

Dormant That period of inactivity, often in winter, when a plant's top growth has withered and no changes appear to occur. Compare *Resting*.

Dwarf A plant naturally smaller than those of the same species, usually taking some years to achieve its ultimate stature.

Epiphyte (Air plant) A plant, growing in the wild, that lives not in soil but on another plant or in rocks. Epiphytes are not parasites, but take sustenance from the atmosphere or decaying debris that has collected in crevices on the host plant or rock.

Growing point The uppermost tip of a stem, where growth is usual.

Hardy Refers to plants that can survive outside throughout the year. Although some hardy plants can be kept indoors for a short period of time, they will not stay healthy if kept at too high a temperature permanently. Compare *Tender*.

Hybrid A plant created from the cross-fertilization of two unlike parents.

Node The point on a stem where leaves and sideshoots develop. Sometimes called a joint.

Offset A young plant produced by a mature specimen that can be detached from its parent for propagation purposes.

Perennial A plant that lives for at least three seasons, usually many more. Compare *Annual* and *Biennial*.

Potting mix Specially prepared soil, usually of peat, loam, perlite and sand in varying quantities, with added fertilizers and always free of weed seeds.

Resting (Rest period) Period when a plant is largely inactive, retaining its foliage but not making new growth. Compare *Dormant*.

Rhizome A fleshy stem that acts as a storage organ, lasting for more than one season, usually horizontal and underground.

Seed-sowing mix Specially prepared soil of similar ingredients to *Potting mix* but usually more finely sieved and with less fertilizer.

Shrub A small, compact plant with woody branches, usually growing from the base rather than from a stem.

Stolon A ground-hugging shoot that, if unchecked, roots and produces another plant.

Succulent A plant bearing fleshy stems and leaves that act as organs for storing water.

Sucker A shoot from the root of a plant that develops roots and top growth of its own.

Tender Refers to plants susceptible to cold; most house plants within the temperate zone are tender. Compare *Hardy*.

Trifoliate Leaf comprising three leaflets.

Tuber A storage organ, often a swollen stem, providing food for a plant during periods of cold or drought.

Variegated Refers to parts of a plant (often leaves) patterned in a color (usually white) other than the basic green.

Index

A

Abutilon 18
Achimenes 19
Aechmea 20
Aeschynanthus 21
African hemp 86
African violet 82
Aloe 22
Amaryllis 55
Anthurium 23
Aphelandra 24
Aporocactus 25

B

Begonia 26
Billbergia 27

Bleeding-glory-vine 36
Bougainvillea 28
Browallia 29
Brunfelsia 30
Busy Lizzy 58
Buying house plants 7

C

Calceolaria 31
Campanula 32
Cape cowslip 65
Catharanthus 33
Cigar flower 40
Cineraria 34
Citrus 35
Clerodendrum 36

Clivia 37
Columnea 38
Crossandra 39
Cuphea 40
Cupid's bower 19
Cuttings, corm
    of *Gesneria* 5
Cuttings, leaf 13
    of *Sinningia* 84
    of *Streptocarpus* 89
Cuttings, leaf bud
    of *Dipladenia* 43
Cuttings, stem 11
    of *Abutilon* 18
    of *Aeschynanthus* 21
    of *Aphelandra* 24

of *Aporocactus* 25
of *Tibouchina* 90
Cuttings, shoot
of *Cuphea* 40
of *Cytisus* 42
of *Punica* 77
Cuttings, tuber
of *Begonia* 26
Cyclamen 41
Cytisus 42

D
Daffodil 69
Dipladenia 43
Diseases
  See Pests and diseases
Division 14
of *Anthurium* 23
of *Billbergia* 27
of *Campanula* 32
of *Liriope* 67

E
Echeveria 44
Epiphyllum 45
Episcia 46
Euphorbia 47
Exacum 48

F
Fairy primrose 76
Falling stars 32
Feeding 8
Fireball lily 53
Flame of the woods 59
Florists' cyclamen 41
Flowering maple 18
Fuchsia 49

G
Gardenia 50
German violet 48
Gesneria 51
Gloriosa 52
Gloxinia 84

H
Haemanthus 53
Hanging-basket
  for *Columnea* 38
  for *Ruellia* 81
Hibiscus 54
Hippeastrum 55
Hot water plant 19
Hoya 56
Humidity 8
  for *Rhododendron* 79
  for *Schlumbergera* 83
Hyacinthus 57

I
Impatiens 58
Indian azalea 79
Italian bellflower 32
Ixora 59

J
Jacobinia 60
Jasminum 61
Jungle geranium 59
Justicia 62

K
Kaffir lily 37
Kalanchoe 63
Kohleria 64

L
Lachenalia 65
Lantana 66
Layering 13
Light, need for 6
Liriope 67

M
Madagascar periwinkle 33
Manettia 68
Monkey-faced pansy 19

N
Narcissus 69

O
Offsets, taking 14
of *Aechmea* 20
of *Aloe* 22
of *Clivia* 37
of *Haemanthus* 53
of *Veltheimia* 93
of *Zantedeschia* 94

P
Pachystachys 70
Passiflora 71
Patient Lucy 58
Pelargonium × *domesticum* 72
Pelargonium × *hortorum* 73
Pentas 74
Persian cyclamen 41
Persian violet 48
Pests and diseases 17
Plumbago 75
Poinsettia 47
Potting mix 10
Potting-on 9
Calceolaria 31
Crossandra 39
Ixora 59

Pricking out
Cineraria 34
Primula 76
Propagation 11
Pruning 16
Punica 77

R
Rebutia 78
Re-potting 9
Rhododendron 79
Rochea 80
Rose periwinkle 33
Ruellia 81

S
Saintpaulia 82
Scarborough lily 92
Schlumbergera 83
Seed, sowing 15
Catharanthus 33
Shrimp plant 62
Sinningia 84
Smithiantha 85
Sparmannia 86
Spathiphyllum 87
Stephanotis 88
Streptocarpus 89
Supports 16
for *Clerodendrum* 36
for *Hoya* 56
for *Jasminum* 61
for *Passiflora* 71
for *Plumbago* 75
for *Stephanotis* 88

T
Temperature 17
Temple bells 85
Tibouchina 90
Top dressing 9
Training 16
Tulipa 91

V
Vallota 92
Veltheimia 93

W
Watering 7

Y
Yellow sage 66
Yesterday-today-and-tomorrow
30

Z
Zantedeschia 94

Acknowledgments
Dorling Kindersley would like to thank Alison Chappel for her special assistance
and the following artists for the illustrations: David Ashby, Vicky Goaman,
Nicki Kemball, Peter Morter, Donald Myall, Sandra Pond, Jim Robins,
Eric Thomas and John Woodcock.

Typesetting
D. P. Media, Hitchin, U.K.